FEB 04

Test Results for Software Write Block Tools: RCMP HDL VO.8

NCJ 203196

Sarah V. Hart
Director

This report was prepared for the National Institute of Justice, U.S. Department of Justice, by the Office of Law Enforcement Standards of the National Institute of Standards and Technology under Interagency Agreement 94–IJ–R–004.

The National Institute of Justice is a component of the Office of Justice Programs, which also includes the Bureau of Justice Assistance, the Bureau of Justice Statistics, the Office of Juvenile Justice and Delinquency Prevention, and the Office for Victims of Crime.

Contents

Introduction

The Computer Forensics Tool Testing (CFTT) program is a joint project of the National Institute of Justice (NIJ), the research and development organization of the U.S. Department of Justice; the National Institute of Standards and Technology's (NIST) Office of Law Enforcement Standards (OLES) and Information Technology Laboratory (ITL); and is supported by other organizations, including the Federal Bureau of Investigation, the Department of Defense Cyber Crime Center, and the Department of Homeland Security's Bureau of Immigration and Customs Enforcement and U.S. Secret Service. The objective of the CFTT project is to provide measurable assurance to practitioners, researchers, and other applicable users that the tools used in computer forensics investigations provide accurate results. Accomplishing this requires the development of specifications and test methods for computer forensics tools and subsequent testing of specific tools against those specifications.

Test results provide the information necessary for developers to improve tools, users to make informed choices, and the legal community and others to understand the tools' capabilities. The approach for testing computer forensic tools is based on well-recognized methodologies for conformance and quality testing. The specifications and test methods are posted on the CFTT Web site (*http://www.cftt.nist.gov*) for both comment and review by the computer forensics community.

This document reports the results from testing the Royal Canadian Mounted Police Hard-Disk Write Lock V0.8 (RCMP HDL) against *Software Write Block Tool Specification & Test Plan, Version 3.0*, available at the CFTT Web site. This specification identifies the top-level tool requirements as—

- The tool shall not allow a protected drive to be changed.
- The tool shall not prevent obtaining any information from or about any drive.
- The tool shall not prevent any operations to a drive that is not protected.

Test Results for Software Write Block Tools: RCMP HDL V0.8

Tool Tested: RCMP HDL V0.8 021126 © RCMP 1993–2002

Operating System: MS DOS (Windows 98 DOS) Version 4.10.2222

Supplier: Royal Canadian Mounted Police
      Technological Crime Branch
      Technical Operations Directorate
Address: 1426 St. Joseph Blvd.
      Ottawa, Ontario K1A 0R2

1. Results Summary by Requirements

The tool shall not allow a protected drive to be changed.
For all test cases run, the tool always blocked commands that would have changed any protected drives.

The tool shall not prevent obtaining any information from or about any drive.
For all test cases run, the tool always allowed commands to obtain information from any protected drives.

The tool shall not prevent any operations to a drive that is not protected.
For all test cases run, the tool always allowed any command to access any unprotected drives.

2. Anomalies

The tool functioned as documented and no anomalies were observed. Two commands in the control category were blocked that could have been allowed: the recalibrate (0x11) and the extended seek (0x47) commands.

Test Cases: SWB-11, SWB-12, SWB-23, and SWB-24.

3. Test Case Selection

The test cases were selected from *Software Write Block Tool Specification & Test Plan, Version 3.0.*

All of the 40 test cases defined in the specification were applied to HDL V0.8.

4. Test Results by Assertion

This section presents the test results grouped by assertion. The assertions are taken from the *Software Write Block Tool Specification & Test Plan, Version 3.0.*

4.1 Mandatory Assertions

SWB-AM-01. **If a drive is protected and a command from the write category is issued for the protected drive, then the tool shall block the command.**

Each command in the write category was sent to all protected drives, and HDL blocked every command sent.

SWB-AM-02. **If a drive is protected and a command from the configuration category is issued for the protected drive then the tool shall block the command.**

Each command in the configuration category was sent to all protected drives, and HDL blocked every command sent.

SWB-AM-03. **If a drive is protected and a command from the miscellaneous category is issued for the protected drive, then the tool shall block the command.**

Each command in the miscellaneous category was sent to all protected drives, and HDL blocked every command sent.

SWB-AM-04. **If a drive is protected and a command from the read category is issued for the protected drive, then the tool shall not block the command.**

Each command in the read category was sent to all protected drives, but HDL never blocked any command sent.

SWM-AM-05. **If a drive is protected and a command from the control category is issued for the protected drive, then the tool shall not block the command.**

Each command in the control category was sent to all protected drives. HDL always blocked two of the commands sent: the recalibrate (0x11) and the extended seek (0x47) commands. HDL never blocked the other commands in the control category.

Test Cases: SWB-11 and SWB-12.

SWB-AM-06. **If a drive is protected and a command from the information category is issued for the protected drive, then the tool shall not block the command.**

Each command in the information category was sent to all protected drives, but HDL never blocked any command sent.

SWB-AM-07. **If the tool is executed, then the tool shall issue a message indicating that the tool is active.**

HDL always issued the message "`Write Lock successfully installed`" to indicate that the tool was active.

SWB-AM-08. **If the tool is executed, then the tool shall issue a message indicating all drives accessible by the covered interfaces.**

HDL always issued the message "`N Hard-Disks reported by Int_13h`" to indicate that N drives were accessible by the interface.

SWB-AM-09. **If the tool is executed, then the tool shall issue a message indicating the protection status of each drive attached to a covered interface.**

For each covered drive, HDL always issued either the messages "`Hard-Disk N Locked!`" or "`Hard-Disk N Not Locked!`" to indicate the protection status of each drive.

SWB-AM-10. **If the tool is configured to return *success* on blocked commands and the tool blocks a command, then the return code shall indicate successful command execution.**

If HDL was configured to return *success* on blocked commands, all blocked commands returned *success*.

SWB-AM-11. **If the tool is configured to return *fail* on blocked commands and the tool blocks a command, then the return code shall indicate unsuccessful command execution.**

If HDL was configured to return *fail* on blocked commands, all blocked commands returned *fail*.

4.2 Optional Assertions

SWB-AO-01. **If a subset of all covered drives is specified for protection, then commands from the write category shall be blocked for drives in the selected subset.**

When a subset of covered drives was selected and each command in the write category was sent to all protected drives, HDL blocked every command sent.

SWB-AO-02. **If a subset of all covered drives is specified for protection, then commands from the configuration category shall be blocked for drives in the selected subset.**

When a subset of covered drives was selected and each command in the configuration category was sent to all protected drives, HDL blocked every command sent.

SWB-AO-03. **If a subset of all covered drives is specified for protection, then commands from the miscellaneous category shall be blocked for drives in the selected subset.**

When a subset of covered drives was selected and each command in the miscellaneous category was sent to all protected drives, HDL blocked every command sent.

SWB-AO-04. **If a subset of all covered drives is specified for protection, then commands from the read category shall not be blocked for drives in the selected subset.**

When a subset of covered drives was selected and each command in the read category was sent to all protected drives, HDL never blocked any command sent.

SWB-AO-05. **If a subset of all covered drives is specified for protection, then commands from the control category shall not be blocked for drives in the selected subset.**

When a subset of covered drives was selected and each command in the control category was sent to all protected drives, HDL always blocked two of the commands sent: the recalibrate (0x11) and the extended seek (0x47) commands. HDL never blocked the other commands in the control category.

Test Cases: SWB-23 and SWB-24.

SWB-AO-06. **If a subset of all covered drives is specified for protection, then commands from the information category shall not be blocked for drives in the selected subset.**

When a subset of covered drives was selected and each command in the information category was sent to all protected drives, HDL never blocked any command sent.

SWB-AO-07. **If a subset of all covered drives is specified for protection, then no commands from any category shall be blocked for drives not in the selected subset.**

When a subset of covered drives was selected and each command in every category was sent to all unprotected drives, HDL never blocked any command sent.

SWB-AO-08. **If the tool is active during the operating system boot and shutdown processes, then no changes are made to any protected drives.**

The system was booted with the test harness and HDL and started from the AUTOEXEC.BAT file. Each command in the write category was sent to every protected drive to show that the tool was active. Finally the system was shut down. A SHA1[1] hash value was then computed and compared to a SHA1 hash value computed before the test for each drive used in the test to ensure that after the harness was no longer active, nothing was written to the drives. The SHA1 hash

---

[1] The Secure Hash Algorithm (SHA1), developed by NIST, along with NSA, for use with the Digital Signature Standard (DSS) is specified within the Secure Hash Standard (SHS) [National Institute of Standards and Technology (NIST). FIPS Publication 180: Secure Hash Standard (SHS). May 1993.]. SHA-1 [National Institute of Standards and Technology (NIST)].

values computed after the test were the same as the values computed before the test, indicating that no changes to the drives occurred during the test.

SWB-AO-09. **If the tool is active and the tool is then deactivated, then no commands to any drive shall be blocked.**

The tool was activated, each command in the write category was sent to each protected drive and then the tool was deactivated. Then when all commands in every category were sent to each drive, HDL never blocked any commands sent.

SWB-AO-10. **If the tool blocks a command, then the tool shall issue either an audio or a visual signal.**

This optional feature is not supported by HDL.

5. Testing Environment

The tests were run in the NIST CFTT lab. This section describes the hardware (test computers and hard drives) available for testing. Not all components were used in testing. The following host computers were used for execution of test cases: Cadfael, Rumpole, Wimsey, JudgeDee, HecRamsey, McCloud, McMillan, and AndWife. Ten hard drives (8 different models, 3 different brands) were used for the tests (Table 5-1).

5.1 Test Computers

Cadfael, Rumpole, Wimsey, and JudgeDee have the following hardware components in common:

Table 5-1. Extended BIOS Host Computer Hardware Components

ASUS CUSL2 Motherboard
BIOS: Award Medallion v6.0
Intel Pentium III (Coppermine) 933Mhz
512,672k Memory
Adaptec 29160N SCSI Adapter card
Plextor CR-RW PX-W124TS Rev: 1.06
Iomega 2GB Jaz drive Rev: E.17
LS-120 Super floppy
Two slots for removable IDE hard disk drives
Two slots for removable SCSI hard disk drive

Rumpole also had a 30GB OnStream SC30 tape drive (not used in the test procedures). JudgeDee had a third slot for a removable IDE hard disk drive.

HecRamsey, McCloud, McMillan, and AndWife have the following hardware components in common (Table 5-2):

Table 5-2. Alternate Extended BIOS Host Computer Hardware Components

Intel D845WNL Motherboard
BIOS: HV84510A.86A.0022.P05
Intel Pentium IV 2.0Ghz
512,672k Memory
Adaptec 29160 SCSI Adapter card
Tekram DC-390U3W SCSI Adapter card
Plextor CR-RW PX-W124TS Rev: 1.06
LG 52X CD-ROM
Floppy drive
Three slots for removable IDE hard disk drives
Two slots for removable SCSI hard disk drive

5.2 Hard Disk Drives

The hard disk drives that were used were selected from the drives listed in Table 5-3. These hard drives were mounted in removable storage modules. Any combination of up to three IDE hard drives and two SCSI hard drives can be installed in Paladin, HecRamsey, McCloud, McMillan, AndWife, Cadfael, Rumpole, Wimsey, or JudgeDee as required for a test. The IDE disks used had jumpers set for cable select. The SCSI ID for the SCSI disks was set to either 0 or 1 as required by the test case.

The hard drives used in testing are described in Table 5-3. The column labeled **Label** is an external identification for the hard drive. The column labeled **Model** is the model identification string obtained from the drive. The **Interface** column identifies the type of interface used to connect the drive to the computer. The **Usable Sectors** column documents the size of the drive in sectors. The column labeled **GB** gives the size of the drive in gigabytes.

Table 5-3. Hard Drives Used in Testing

Label	Model	Interface	Usable Sectors	GB
1F	QUANTUM_ATLAS10K3_18_SCA	SCSI	35916547	18.38
2B	QUANTUM QM39100TD-SCA	SCSI	17783249	9.10
64	WDCWD64AA	IDE	12594960	6.44
6F	Maxtor 6Y060L0	IDE	120103200	61.49
8A	WDC WD200EB-00CSF0	IDE	39102336	20.02
90	WDC WD300BB-00CAA0	IDE	58633344	30.02
E3	QUANTUM ATLAS10K2-TY092J	SCSI	17938985	9.18
E4	QUANTUM ATLAS10K2-TY092J	SCSI	17938985	9.18
F5	IBM-DTLA-307020	IDE	40188960	20.57
F6	IBM-DTLA-307020	IDE	40188960	20.57

The drives are set up in a variety of ways with the common partition types (FAT16, FAT32, FAT32X, NTFS, and Linux ext2) represented. The setup of each drive is documented in Table 5-4. The column labeled **Drive Label** is an external identification for the hard drive. The column labeled **Partition Table** describes the partition table for the drive. In the partition table description the column labeled **N** is a sequence number. The unlabeled column identifies a primary partition (P), a primary extended partition (X), a secondary partition within an extended partition (S), or an extended partition within an extended partition (x). The column labeled **Start LBA** is the starting logical block address (LBA) of the partition. The column labeled **Length** is the length of the partition in sectors. The column labeled **Boot** indicates the boot partition. The column labeled **Partition Type** contains the two-digit hexadecimal partition type code and name of the partition type for common partition types.

Table 5-4. Drive Partition Setup

Drive Label	Partition Table
1F	N Start LBA Length Boot Partition Type 1 P 000000063 001236942 Boot 0B Fat32 2 X 001429785 033865020 0F extended 3 S 000000063 000208782 83 Linux 4 x 000208845 000144585 05 extended 5 S 000000063 000144522 0B Fat32 6 x 000771120 000192780 05 extended 7 S 000000063 000192717 16 other 8 S 000000000 000000000 00 empty entry 9 P 035294805 000064260 83 Linux
2B	No partition table
64	No partition table
6F	No partition table
8A	No partition table
90	No partition table
E3	N Start LBA Length Boot Partition Type 1 P 000000063 071681967 0C Fat32X 2 P 000000000 000000000 00 empty entry 3 P 000000000 000000000 00 empty entry 4 P 000000000 000000000 00 empty entry
E4	N Start LBA Length Boot Partition Type 1 P 000000063 006152832 Boot 0B Fat32 2 X 008193150 009735390 0F extended 3 S 000000000 000000000 00 empty entry 4 x 002056320 001237005 05 extended 5 S 000000063 001236942 07 NTFS 6 x 005349645 001638630 05 extended 7 S 000000063 001638567 17 other 8 x 008498385 001237005 05 extended 9 S 000000063 001236942 1B other
F5	N Start LBA Length Boot Partition Type 1 P 000000063 001236942 Boot 06 Fat16 2 X 002249100 007181055 05 extended 3 S 000000063 000208782 83 Linux 4 x 000208845 000144585 05 extended 5 S 000000063 000144522 06 Fat16 6 x 004450005 000192780 05 extended 7 S 000000063 000192717 16 other 8 S 000000000 000000000 00 empty entry 9 P 009430155 006152895 83 Linux
F6	N Start LBA Length Boot Partition Type 1 P 000000063 006152832 Boot 0B Fat32 2 X 008193150 031985415 0F extended 3 S 000000000 000000000 00 empty entry 4 x 002056320 001237005 05 extended 5 S 000000063 001236942 07 NTFS 6 x 005349645 001638630 05 extended 7 S 000000063 001638567 17 other 8 x 030748410 001237005 05 extended 9 S 000000063 001236942 1B other

After the drives were created, a SHA1 hash value was computed for the entire drive (Table 5-5). After testing was finished, a SHA1 hash value was computed again (Table 5-6). The lack of change in the SHA1 hash values indicates that no changes were made to the drives during testing.

Table 5-5. Drive SHA1 Values Before Testing

Drive	SHA1 Hash Value
1F	7DB8B538BC38907FC22B1CA79996D97F77421418
2B	2A7810E851B7392C3D4836A5DFFB5E73E8295C6F
64	8F52C49579C70407FE6D0EDCBE3FD7C42972823A
6F	7C2F5F4FB0D04E5F1B51D0888753A1B125A503EA
8A	891444D852E0C48C4713952B3BDAD89E03C205FD
90	08B4905B4D012401656248C39C904F6072476293
E3	3B0715864B366D08264441DC7F75082F5EE4C0CC
E4	25BF8AF6B2D3E0BD1909C96E368DB27F51C49CBF
F5	2418FD48F2A94389965E3740303C6160F7F35B5C
F6	8034683D5D55BA51409AC7B5CB0845CA2CF6B235

Table 5-6. Drive SHA1 Values After Testing

Drive	SHA1 Hash Value
1F	7DB8B538BC38907FC22B1CA79996D97F77421418
2B	2A7810E851B7392C3D4836A5DFFB5E73E8295C6F
64	8F52C49579C70407FE6D0EDCBE3FD7C42972823A
6F	7C2F5F4FB0D04E5F1B51D0888753A1B125A503EA
8A	891444D852E0C48C4713952B3BDAD89E03C205FD
90	08B4905B4D012401656248C39C904F6072476293
E3	3B0715864B366D08264441DC7F75082F5EE4C0CC
E4	25BF8AF6B2D3E0BD1909C96E368DB27F51C49CBF
F5	2418FD48F2A94389965E3740303C6160F7F35B5C
F6	8034683D5D55BA51409AC7B5CB0845CA2CF6B235

5.3 Support Software

Software Write Block Test Harness (SWBT) Release 1.0 was developed to support the testing of interrupt 13h-based software write block tools. The program DISKWIPE from the FS-TST Release 1.0 package was used in the drive setup procedure. Both FS-TST Release 1.0 and SWBT Release 1.0 can be obtained from *http://www.cftt.nist.gov*. The support software has components to monitor interrupt 13 activity (TALLY13.COM) and to issue each of the 256 possible interrupt 13 commands (TEST-HDL.EXE). The TEST-HDL program was written in ANSI C and compiled with the Borland C++ compiler version 4.5. The TALLY13 program was written in assembler language and compiled with Borland Turbo Assembler version 5.0. The programs listed in Table 5-7 are required for testing.

Table 5-7. Software Required for Testing

Program	Description
SWB Tool	The software write block tool to be tested.
TALLY13	The interrupt 0x13 monitor program. The monitor program blocks all

Program	Description
	interrupt 0x13 command functions, counts the number of times each function is requested for each drive, and provides an interface for retrieving the count of the number of times each command function was requested for each drive.
TEST-HDL	The test harness issues (requests) all interrupt 0x13 command functions for a specified command category, queries the monitor program to determine if the function was blocked or allowed, and then logs the results to a file.
T-OFF	Deactivate TALLY13.

5.4 Run Protocol Selection

Most test cases follow the same test procedures. However, some test cases require a special procedure. The procedure for setting up a selection of hard drives for use in testing is as follows:

1. Select a hard drive.
2. Use the FS-TST diskwipe program to initialize the drive.
3. Create and format partitions on the drive (optional step).
4. Compute a reference SHA1 hash of the drive.

The general procedure for executing a test case is as follows:

1. Select a test case to execute.
2. Install the number of hard drives called for by the test case.
3. Boot the test computer into DOS.
4. Follow the run protocol for the selected test case.
5. Save test case results to an archive location.

The **run protocol** specifies the actual procedures to follow for the test case. Some test cases require different setup procedures and methods to measure results. The values for test parameters such as **return type, command category, N drives,** and **protection pattern** can be found in *Software Write Block Tool Specification & Test Plan, Version 3.0.* The following protocols are defined:

- Typical
  1. Execute the interrupt 0x13 monitor (TALLY13).
  2. Execute the SWB tool under test with the specified **return type**.
  3. Execute TEST-HDL for the specified **command category**.
- Uninstall
  1. Execute the interrupt 0x13 monitor (TALLY13).
  2. Execute the SWB tool under test with the specified **return** type.
  3. Execute TEST-HDL for the **write** command category.
  4. Execute T-OFF to deactivate TALLY13.
  5. Uninstall the SWB tool.
  6. Execute TEST-HDL for each **command category**.

- Boot
  1. Install the SWB tool. (For DOS systems, include the tool and monitor in the **AUTOEXEC.BAT** file.)
  2. Boot the system.
  3. Execute TEST-HDL for the **write** command category.
  4. Shutdown the system.

The **typical** protocol applies to cases 01–36, the **boot** protocol applies to test cases 37 and 38, and the **uninstall** protocol applies to cases 39 and 40.

6. Interpretation of Test Results

The main item of interest for interpretation of the test results is determining the conformance of the tool to the test assertions. This section lists each test assertion and identifies the information in the log files relevant to conformance with the assertion. Conformance of each assertion tested by a given test case is evaluated by examination of the Commands Executed and the Log File Highlights boxes of the test report summary.

6.1 Test Assertion Verification

This section describes where to find the information needed to verify each test assertion in the test case report.

SWB-AM-01.   **If a drive is protected and a command from the write category is issued for the protected drive, then the tool shall block the command.**

The protected drives are identified on the HDL command line in the Commands Executed box. The Test Harness Log lists each command sent to each drive. If the action column contains *blocked* for each command sent to a protected drive, the test case conforms to the assertion.

SWB-AM-02.   **If a drive is protected and a command from the configuration category is issued for the protected drive, then the tool shall block the command.**

The protected drives are identified on the HDL command line in the Commands Executed box. The Test Harness Log lists each command sent to each drive. If the action column contains *blocked* for each command sent to a protected drive, the test case conforms to the assertion.

SWB-AM-03.   **If a drive is protected and a command from the miscellaneous category is issued for the protected drive, then the tool shall block the command.**

The protected drives are identified on the HDL command line in the Commands Executed box. The Test Harness Log lists each command sent to each drive. If the action column contains *blocked* for each command sent to a protected drive, the test case conforms to the assertion.

SWB-AM-04. **If a drive is protected and a command from the read category is issued for the protected drive, then the tool shall not block the command.**

The protected drives are identified on the HDL command line in the Commands Executed box. The Test Harness Log lists each command sent to each drive. If the action column contains *allowed* for each command sent to a protected drive, the test case conforms to the assertion.

SWB-AM-05. **If a drive is protected and a command from the control category is issued for the protected drive, then the tool shall not block the command.**

The protected drives are identified on the HDL command line in the Commands Executed box. The Test Harness Log lists each command sent to each drive. If the action column contains *allowed* for each command sent to a protected drive, the test case conforms to the assertion.

SWB-AM-06. **If a drive is protected and a command from the information category is issued for the protected drive, then the tool shall not block the command.**

The protected drives are identified on the HDL command line in the Commands Executed box. The Test Harness Log lists each command sent to each drive. If the action column contains *allowed* for each command sent to a protected drive, the test case conforms to the assertion.

SWB-AM-07. **If the tool is executed, then the tool shall issue a message indicating that the tool is active.**

If the Install HDL Log contains the text: "Write Lock successfully installed," then the test case conforms to the test assertion.

SWB-AM-08. **If the tool is executed, then the tool shall issue a message indicating all drives accessible by the covered interfaces.**

HDL always issued the message "N Hard-Disks reported by Int_13h" to indicate that N drives were accessible by the interface. If N is the same as the number of drives specified on the TEST-HDL command line in the Commands Executed box, then the test case is in conformance with the test assertion.

SWB-AM-09. **If the tool is executed, then the tool shall issue a message indicating the protection status of each drive attached to a covered interface.**

For each covered drive, HDL always issued either the messages "Hard-Disk N Locked!" or "Hard-Disk N Not Locked!" to indicate the protection status of each drive. If drive N is listed on the command line to HDL and the Install HDL log reports drive N as locked, then the test case is in conformance with the test assertion.

SWB-AM-10. **If the tool is configured to return** *success* **on blocked commands and the tool blocks a command, then the return code shall indicate successful command execution.**

HDL was configured to return *success* on blocked commands if an S flag was used on the HDL command line. The return value of blocked commands is *success* if in the Test Harness Log the value of the stat column is 0000 and the value of the Cry column is off.

SWB-AM-11. **If the tool is configured to return** *fail* **on blocked commands and the tool blocks a command, then the return code shall indicate unsuccessful command execution.**

HDL was configured to return *fail* on blocked commands if no S flag was used on the HDL command line. The return value of blocked commands is *fail* if in the Test Harness Log the value of the stat column is 0300 and the value of the Cry column is on.

SWB-AO-01. **If a subset of all covered drives is specified for protection, then commands from the write category shall be blocked for drives in the selected subset.**

The protected drives are identified on the HDL command line in the Commands Executed box. The Test Harness Log lists each command sent to each drive. If the action column contains *blocked* for each command sent to a protected drive, the test case conforms to the assertion.

SWB-AO-02. **If a subset of all covered drives is specified for protection, then commands from the configuration category shall be blocked for drives in the selected subset.**

The protected drives are identified on the HDL command line in the Commands Executed box. The Test Harness Log lists each command sent to each drive. If the action column contains *blocked* for each command sent to a protected drive, the test case conforms to the assertion.

SWB-AO-03. **If a subset of all covered drives is specified for protection, then commands from the miscellaneous category shall be blocked for drives in the selected subset.**

The protected drives are identified on the HDL command line in the Commands Executed box. The Test Harness Log lists each command sent to each drive. If the action column contains *blocked* for each command sent to a protected drive, the test case conforms to the assertion.

SWB-AO-04. **If a subset of all covered drives is specified for protection, then commands from the read category shall not be blocked for drives in the selected subset.**

The protected drives are identified on the HDL command line in the Commands Executed box. The Test Harness Log lists each command sent to each drive. If the action column contains *allowed* for each command sent to a protected drive, the test case conforms to the assertion.

SWB-AO-05. **If a subset of all covered drives is specified for protection, then commands from the control category shall not be blocked for drives in the selected subset.**

The protected drives are identified on the HDL command line in the Commands Executed box. The Test Harness Log lists each command sent to each drive. If the action column contains *allowed* for each command sent to a protected drive, the test case conforms to the assertion.

SWB-AO-06. **If a subset of all covered drives is specified for protection, then commands from the information category shall not be blocked for drives in the selected subset.**

The protected drives are identified on the HDL command line in the Commands Executed box. The Test Harness Log lists each command sent to each drive. If the action column contains *allowed* for each command sent to a protected drive, the test case conforms to the assertion.

SWB-AO-07. **If a subset of all covered drives is specified for protection, then no commands from any category shall be blocked for drives not in the selected subset.**

The protected drives are identified on the HDL command line in the Commands Executed box. The unprotected drives are the drives not listed on the HDL command line. The Test Harness Log lists each command sent to each drive. If the action column contains *allowed* for each command sent to an unprotected drive, the test case conforms to the assertion.

SWB-AO-08. **If the tool is active during the operating system boot and shutdown processes, then no changes are made to any protected drives.**

The protected drives are identified on the HDL command line in the Commands Executed box. The Test Harness Log lists each command sent to each drive. If the action column contains *blocked* for each command sent to a protected drive, the test case conforms to the assertion.

SWB-AO-09. **If the tool is active and the tool is then deactivated, then no commands to any drive shall be blocked.**

This assertion requires a special test protocol. In the first part of the test, the tool is activated and some write commands are blocked. In the second part of the test, the tool is deactivated and every command is sent to all installed drives. There are two log files for the tool and two log files for the test harness. The tool is allowed to refuse to deactivate. The tool refuses to deactivate if the tool has been configured to return *success* for blocked commands since deactivation might allow a buffered write to take place. If the tool is successfully deactivated, then all commands are allowed to all drives. If the tool does not deactivate, then no change occurs to the protection status of the drives.

A warning message appears in the second instance of the Test Harness Log file. This is normal for test cases SWB-39 and SWB-40. The warning message notes that write commands were allowed to unprotected drives while the tool was active during the first part of the test before the tool was deactivated.

SWB-AO-10.   **If the tool blocks a command, then the tool shall issue either an audio or a visual signal.**

This optional feature is not supported by HDL.

6.2 Test Results Summary Key

A summary of the actual test results is presented in this report. Table 6-1 presents a description of each section of the test results summary.

Table 6-1. Description of Test Report Summary

Heading	Description
First Line:	Test case ID and name and version of software tested.
Case Summary:	Test case summary from *Software Write Block Tool Specification & Test Plan, Version 3.0.*
Assertions Tested:	The test assertions tested by the test case from *Software Write Block Tool Specification & Test Plan, Version 3.0.*
Tester Name:	Name or initials of person executing test procedure.
Test Date:	Time and date that test was started.
Test PC:	Name of computer where the tool under test was executed.
Test Software:	The name and version of the test software.
Hard Drives Used:	Description of the hard drives used in the test.
Commands Executed:	Documentation of each command executed during the test. The protected drives are identified on the HDL command line. HDL identifies the drives starting at 0.
Log File Highlights:	Selected entries from the test case log files. There are three log files that may appear. The log file created for TALLY13 is labeled *Monitor Execution.* The log file created for HDL is labeled *Install HDL Log.* The log file created by TEST-HDL is labeled *Test Harness Log.* For test cases SWB-39 and SWB-40, there are two separate logs for HDL and also for TEST-HDL because these cases require execution of HDL twice. The Monitor Execution log file records the program version and the date that the TALLY13 program was executed. The HDL log file is obtained by output redirection of the execution of HDL. The log file contains the version of HDL used (V0.8), the number of drives identified, and the protection status of each drive. The Test Harness Log is the record of commands sent to HDL and the action taken by HDL to either block or allow

Heading	Description
	each command sent. The format of the file is as follows: 1. Command line: The command line used to execute TEST-HDL. This line begins with the string CMD. 2. Case number. 3. Interrupt 0x13 Functions: The category of interrupt 0x13 functions tested by this case. 4. Date. 5. Version: Version information about TEST-HDL and components. The creation date, creation time, and version of each source code component is listed. The compile time and date for the executable program is listed. 6. Operator: The operator running the test. 7. Host: The host computer running the test. 8. Drives: The number of drives and the external drive label for each drive. The next two items are repeated for each installed drive. 9. List of commands sent: Each line of the list has 9 columns: sequence number, test case number, command code in hex (Cmd), drive number in hex (Drv), action taken by HDL (either *blocked* or *allowed*), return status (0000 means success, 0300 means fail), carry flag value (labeled Cry with values of either *on* indicating failure status, or *off* indicating success status), count of the number of times the command was allowed by HDL, and the command name (or undefined for commands in the miscellaneous category). 10. Summary of commands for the drive: The message indicates the number of commands blocked out of the number of commands sent. 11. The last item is a summary of all the commands sent to all drives, the number of commands sent, the number blocked, and the number allowed (not blocked).
Results:	Expected and actual results for each assertion tested.
Analysis:	Whether or not the expected results were achieved.

7. Test Results Summaries

Case SWB-01 HDL -- Int_13 Hard Disk Write Lock V0.8 021126 © RCMP 1993-2002	
Case Summary:	SWB-01 Install all drives, configure return code to failure, protect all drives, execute write commands.
Assertions Tested:	SWB-AM-01. If a drive is protected and a command from the write category is issued for the protected drive then the tool shall block the command. SWB-AM-07. If the tool is executed then the tool shall issue a message indicating that the tool is active. SWB-AM-08. If the tool is executed then the tool shall issue a message indicating all drives accessible by the covered interfaces. SWB-AM-09. If the tool is executed then the tool shall issue a message indicating the protection status of each drive attached to a covered interface. SWB-AM-11. If the tool is configured to return fail on blocked commands and the tool blocks a command then the return code shall indicate unsuccessful command execution.
Tester Name:	JRL
Test Date:	Sun Aug 31 09:26:28 2003
Test PC:	Wimsey
Test Software:	SWBT 1.0
Hard Drives Used:	Drive 80, label 90 is a WDC WD300BB-00CAA0 with 58633344 sectors Drive 81, label 8A is a WDC WD200EB-00CSF0 with 39102336 sectors Drive 82, label E4 is a QUANTUM ATLAS10K2-TY092J with 17938985 sectors Drive 83, label 2B is a Quantum QM39100TD-SCA Drive with 17783249 sectors
Commands Executed:	Boot Test PC to (DOS 7.1) Windows 98 [Version 4.10.2222] tally13 hdl8 0123 test-hdl SWB-01 Wimsey JRL w 90 8A E4 2B Shutdown Test PC

Log File Highlights:	***** Monitor Execution *****
	Monitor BIOS interrupt 13h (disk service)
	tally13 compiled on 07/29/03 at 07:33:17
	@(#) Version 1.1 Created 07/29/03 at 07:28:05
	Now (08/31/03 at 09:26:25) Going . . . TSR
	***** Install HDL Log *****
	HDL -- Int_13 Hard Disk Write Lock V0.8 021126 (c)RCMP 1993-2002
	    ---- Royal Canadian Mounted Police ----
	    UNAUTHORIZED USE / DISTRIBUTION PROHIBITED
	
	    Licensee: US Dept. Commerce / NIST S/W Testing
	    4 Hard-Disks reported by Int_13h
	    Hard-Disk 0 Locked!
	    Hard-Disk 1 Locked!
	    Hard-Disk 2 Locked!
	    Hard-Disk 3 Locked!
	    Write Lock successfully installed.
	***** Test Harness Log *****
	CMD: A:\TEST-HDL.EXE SWB-01 Wimsey JRL w 90 8A E4 2B
	Case: SWB-01
	Command set: Write
	Date: Sun Aug 31 09:26:28 2003
	
	Version: @(#) test-hdl.cpp Version 1.1 Created 08/23/03 at 10:13:51
	    @(#) wb-defs.h Version 1.2 Created 08/31/03 at 08:18:19
	    Compiled on Aug 31 2003 at 08:10:54
	Operator: JRL
	Host: Wimsey
	Number of drives 4, Drives: 90 8A E4 2B
	    Case Cmd Drv Action Stat Cry Count Cmd Name
	  0 SWB-01 <03> 80 Blocked 0300 On 0 WriteSectors
	  1 SWB-01 <0B> 80 Blocked 0300 On 0 WriteLong
	  2 SWB-01 <43> 80 Blocked 0300 On 0 ExtWrite
	Results for SWB-01 category w on drive 80 All commands blocked (3 of 3)
	  0 SWB-01 <03> 81 Blocked 0300 On 0 WriteSectors
	  1 SWB-01 <0B> 81 Blocked 0300 On 0 WriteLong
	  2 SWB-01 <43> 81 Blocked 0300 On 0 ExtWrite
	Results for SWB-01 category w on drive 81 All commands blocked (3 of 3)
	  0 SWB-01 <03> 82 Blocked 0300 On 0 WriteSectors
	  1 SWB-01 <0B> 82 Blocked 0300 On 0 WriteLong

	2 SWB-01 <43> 82 Blocked 0300 On 0 ExtWrite
	Results for SWB-01 category w on drive 82 All commands blocked (3 of 3)
	  0 SWB-01 <03> 83 Blocked 0300 On 0 WriteSectors
	  1 SWB-01 <0B> 83 Blocked 0300 On 0 WriteLong
	  2 SWB-01 <43> 83 Blocked 0300 On 0 ExtWrite
	Results for SWB-01 category w on drive 83 All commands blocked (3 of 3)
	Summary: 12 sent, 12 blocked, 0 not blocked

Results:			
	Assertion	**Expected Results**	**Actual Results**
	AM-01	All cmds to drive 80 blocked	All cmds to drive 80 blocked
	AM-01	All cmds to drive 81 blocked	All cmds to drive 81 blocked
	AM-01	All cmds to drive 82 blocked	All cmds to drive 82 blocked
	AM-01	All cmds to drive 83 blocked	All cmds to drive 83 blocked
	AM-07	Tool active message	Tool active message
	AM-08	4 drives identified	4 drives identified
	AM-09	Drive 80 is protected	Drive 80 is protected
	AM-09	Drive 81 is protected	Drive 81 is protected
	AM-09	Drive 82 is protected	Drive 82 is protected
	AM-09	Drive 83 is protected	Drive 83 is protected
	AM-11	12 Commands return fail	12 Commands return fail

Analysis:	SWB-01 Expected results achieved

Case SWB-02 HDL -- Int_13 Hard Disk Write Lock V0.8 021126 © RCMP 1993-2002

Case Summary:	SWB-02 Install two drives, configure return code to success, protect all drives, execute write commands.
Assertions Tested:	SWB-AM-01. If a drive is protected and a command from the write category is issued for the protected drive then the tool shall block the command. SWB-AM-07. If the tool is executed then the tool shall issue a message indicating that the tool is active. SWB-AM-08. If the tool is executed then the tool shall issue a message indicating all drives accessible by the covered interfaces. SWB-AM-09. If the tool is executed then the tool shall issue a message indicating the protection status of each drive attached to a covered interface. SWB-AM-10. If the tool is configured to return success on blocked commands and the tool blocks a command then the return code shall indicate successful command execution.
Tester Name:	JRL
Test Date:	Sun Aug 31 08:55:14 2003
Test PC:	Wimsey
Test Software:	SWBT 1.0
Hard Drives Used:	Drive 80, label 90 is a WDC WD300BB-00CAA0 with 58633344 sectors Drive 81, label 64 is a WDC WD64AA with 12594960 sectors
Commands Executed:	Boot Test PC to (DOS 7.1) Windows 98 [Version 4.10.2222] tally13 hdl8 S01 test-hdl SWB-02 Wimsey JRL w 90 64 Shutdown Test PC

Log File Highlights:	***** Monitor Execution *****
	Monitor BIOS interrupt 13h (disk service)
	tally13 compiled on 07/29/03 at 07:33:17
	@(#) Version 1.1 Created 07/29/03 at 07:28:05
	Now (08/31/03 at 08:55:12) Going . . . TSR
	***** Install HDL Log *****
	HDL -- Int_13 Hard Disk Write Lock V0.8 021126 (c)RCMP 1993-2002
	   ---- Royal Canadian Mounted Police ----
	   UNAUTHORIZED USE / DISTRIBUTION PROHIBITED
	
	   Licensee: US Dept. Commerce / NIST S/W Testing
	   2 Hard-Disks reported by Int_13h
	   Hard-Disk 0 Locked!
	   Hard-Disk 1 Locked!
	   Write Lock successfully installed.

```
***** Test Harness Log *****
CMD: A:\TEST-HDL.EXE SWB-02 Wimsey JRL w 90 64
Case: SWB-02
Command set: Write
Date: Sun Aug 31 08:55:14 2003

Version: @(#) test-hdl.cpp Version 1.1 Created 08/23/03 at 10:13:51
         @(#) wb-defs.h Version 1.2 Created 08/31/03 at 08:18:19
         Compiled on Aug 31 2003 at 08:10:54
Operator: JRL
Host: Wimsey
Number of drives 2, Drives: 90 64
     Case  Cmd Drv Action  Stat Cry Count Cmd Name
  0  SWB-02 <03> 80 Blocked 0000 Off     0  WriteSectors
  1  SWB-02 <0B> 80 Blocked 0000 Off     0  WriteLong
  2  SWB-02 <43> 80 Blocked 0000 Off     0  ExtWrite
Results for SWB-02 category w on drive 80 All commands blocked (3 of 3)
  0  SWB-02 <03> 81 Blocked 0000 Off     0  WriteSectors
  1  SWB-02 <0B> 81 Blocked 0000 Off     0  WriteLong
  2  SWB-02 <43> 81 Blocked 0000 Off     0  ExtWrite
Results for SWB-02 category w on drive 81 All commands blocked (3 of 3)
Summary: 6 sent, 6 blocked, 0 not blocked
```

Results:			
	Assertion	**Expected Results**	**Actual Results**
	AM-01	All cmds to drive 80 blocked	All cmds to drive 80 blocked
	AM-01	All cmds to drive 81 blocked	All cmds to drive 81 blocked
	AM-07	Tool active message	Tool active message
	AM-08	2 drives identified	2 drives identified
	AM-09	Drive 80 is protected	Drive 80 is protected
	AM-09	Drive 81 is protected	Drive 81 is protected
	AM-10	6 Commands return success	6 Commands return success

Analysis:	SWB-02 Expected results achieved

Case SWB-03 HDL -- Int_13 Hard Disk Write Lock V0.8 021126 © RCMP 1993-2002

Case Summary:	SWB-03 Install one drive, configure return code to failure, protect all drives, execute configuration commands.
Assertions Tested:	SWB-AM-02. If a drive is protected and a command from the configuration category is issued for the protected drive then the tool shall block the command. SWB-AM-07. If the tool is executed then the tool shall issue a message indicating that the tool is active. SWB-AM-08. If the tool is executed then the tool shall issue a message indicating all drives accessible by the covered interfaces. SWB-AM-09. If the tool is executed then the tool shall issue a message indicating the protection status of each drive attached to a covered interface. SWB-AM-11. If the tool is configured to return fail on blocked commands and the tool blocks a command then the return code shall indicate unsuccessful command execution.
Tester Name:	JRL
Test Date:	Sun Aug 31 09:00:42 2003
Test PC:	McCloud
Test Software:	SWBT 1.0
Hard Drives Used:	Drive 80, label 8A is a WDC WD200EB-00CSF0 with 39102336 sectors
Commands Executed:	Boot Test PC to (DOS 7.1) Windows 98 [Version 4.10.2222] tally13 hdl8 0 test-hdl SWB-03 McCloud JRL x 8A Shutdown Test PC
Log File Highlights:	***** Monitor Execution ***** Monitor BIOS interrupt 13h (disk service) tally13 compiled on 07/29/03 at 07:33:17 @(#) Version 1.1 Created 07/29/03 at 07:28:05 Now (08/31/03 at 09:00:35) Going . . . TSR ***** Install HDL Log *****

```
        HDL -- Int_13 Hard Disk Write Lock V0.8 021126 (c)RCMP 1993-2002
                 ---- Royal Canadian Mounted Police ----
             UNAUTHORIZED USE / DISTRIBUTION PROHIBITED

             Licensee: US Dept. Commerce / NIST S/W Testing
             1 Hard-Disks reported by Int_13h
             Hard-Disk 0     Locked!
             Write Lock successfully installed.
     ***** Test Harness Log *****
     CMD: A:\TEST-HDL.EXE SWB-03 McCloud JRL x 8A
     Case: SWB-03
     Command set: Configure
     Date: Sun Aug 31 09:00:42 2003

     Version: @(#) test-hdl.cpp Version 1.1 Created 08/23/03 at 10:13:51
              @(#) wb-defs.h Version 1.2 Created 08/31/03 at 08:18:19
              Compiled on Aug 31 2003 at 08:10:54
     Operator: JRL
     Host: McCloud
     Number of drives 1, Drives: 8A
             Case  Cmd Drv Action Stat Cry Count Cmd Name
       0 SWB-03 <05> 80 Blocked 0300 On      0  FormatTrack
       1 SWB-03 <06> 80 Blocked 0300 On      0  FormatBadSectors
       2 SWB-03 <07> 80 Blocked 0300 On      0  FormatCyl
       3 SWB-03 <09> 80 Blocked 0300 On      0  InitDriveParms
       4 SWB-03 <0E> 80 Blocked 0300 On      0  DiagnosticESDI
       5 SWB-03 <0F> 80 Blocked 0300 On      0  DiagnosticESDI
       6 SWB-03 <12> 80 Blocked 0300 On      0  DiagnosticRAM
       7 SWB-03 <13> 80 Blocked 0300 On      0  DiagnosticDrive
       8 SWB-03 <14> 80 Blocked 0300 On      0  DiagnosticCTL
     Results for SWB-03 category x on drive 80 All commands blocked (9 of 9)
     Summary: 9 sent, 9 blocked, 0 not blocked
```

Results:			
	Assertion	**Expected Results**	**Actual Results**
	AM-02	All cmds to drive 80 blocked	All cmds to drive 80 blocked
	AM-07	Tool active message	Tool active message
	AM-08	1 drive identified	1 drive identified
	AM-09	Drive 80 is protected	Drive 80 is protected
	AM-11	9 Commands return fail	9 Commands return fail
Analysis:	SWB-03 Expected results achieved		

Case Summary:	SWB-04 Install all drives, configure return code to success, protect all drives, execute configuration commands.
Assertions Tested:	SWB-AM-02. If a drive is protected and a command from the configuration category is issued for the protected drive then the tool shall block the command. SWB-AM-07. If the tool is executed then the tool shall issue a message indicating that the tool is active. SWB-AM-08. If the tool is executed then the tool shall issue a message indicating all drives accessible by the covered interfaces. SWB-AM-09. If the tool is executed then the tool shall issue a message indicating the protection status of each drive attached to a covered interface. SWB-AM-10. If the tool is configured to return success on blocked commands and the tool blocks a command then the return code shall indicate successful command execution.
Tester Name:	JRL
Test Date:	Sun Aug 31 09:29:00 2003
Test PC:	HecRamsey
Test Software:	SWBT 1.0
Hard Drives Used:	Drive 80, label F5 is an IBM-DTLA-307020 with 40188960 sectors Drive 81, label 64 is a WDC WD64AA with 12594960 sectors Drive 82, label 6F is a Maxtor 6Y060L0 with 120103200 sectors Drive 83, label E3 is a QUANTUM ATLAS10K2-TY092J with 17938985 sectors Drive 84, label 1F is a Quantum ATLAS10K3_18_SCA Drive with 35916548 sectors

Case SWB-04 HDL -- Int_13 Hard Disk Write Lock V0.8 021126 © RCMP 1993-2002	
Commands Executed:	Boot Test PC to (DOS 7.1) Windows 98 [Version 4.10.2222] tally13 hdl8 S01234 test-hdl SWB-04 HecRamsey JRL x F5 64 6F E3 1F Shutdown Test PC

Log File Highlights:	***** Monitor Execution *****
	Monitor BIOS interrupt 13h (disk service)
	tally13 compiled on 07/29/03 at 07:33:17
	@(#) Version 1.1 Created 07/29/03 at 07:28:05
	Now (08/31/03 at 09:28:53) Going . . . TSR
	***** Install HDL Log *****
	HDL -- Int_13 Hard Disk Write Lock V0.8 021126 (c)RCMP 1993-2002
	      ---- Royal Canadian Mounted Police ----
	      UNAUTHORIZED USE / DISTRIBUTION PROHIBITED
	
	      Licensee: US Dept. Commerce / NIST S/W Testing
	      5 Hard-Disks reported by Int_13h
	      Hard-Disk 0 Locked!
	      Hard-Disk 1 Locked!
	      Hard-Disk 2 Locked!
	      Hard-Disk 3 Locked!
	      Hard-Disk 4 Locked!
	      Write Lock successfully installed.
	***** Test Harness Log *****
	CMD: A:\TEST-HDL.EXE SWB-04 HecRamsey JRL x F5 64 6F E3 1F
	Case: SWB-04
	Command set: Configure
	Date: Sun Aug 31 09:29:00 2003
	
	Version: @(#) test-hdl.cpp Version 1.1 Created 08/23/03 at 10:13:51
	      @(#) wb-defs.h Version 1.2 Created 08/31/03 at 08:18:19
	      Compiled on Aug 31 2003 at 08:10:54
	Operator: JRL
	Host: HecRamsey
	Number of drives 5, Drives: F5 64 6F E3 1F

```
      Case  Cmd Drv Action  Stat Cry Count Cmd Name
 0 SWB-04 <05> 80 Blocked 0000 Off    0  FormatTrack
 1 SWB-04 <06> 80 Blocked 0000 Off    0  FormatBadSectors
 2 SWB-04 <07> 80 Blocked 0000 Off    0  FormatCyl
 3 SWB-04 <09> 80 Blocked 0000 Off    0  InitDriveParms
 4 SWB-04 <0E> 80 Blocked 0000 Off    0  DiagnosticESDI
 5 SWB-04 <0F> 80 Blocked 0000 Off    0  DiagnosticESDI
 6 SWB-04 <12> 80 Blocked 0000 Off    0  DiagnosticRAM
 7 SWB-04 <13> 80 Blocked 0000 Off    0  DiagnosticDrive
 8 SWB-04 <14> 80 Blocked 0000 Off    0  DiagnosticCTL
Results for SWB-04 category x on drive 80 All commands blocked (9 of 9)
 0 SWB-04 <05> 81 Blocked 0000 Off    0  FormatTrack
 1 SWB-04 <06> 81 Blocked 0000 Off    0  FormatBadSectors
 2 SWB-04 <07> 81 Blocked 0000 Off    0  FormatCyl
 3 SWB-04 <09> 81 Blocked 0000 Off    0  InitDriveParms
 4 SWB-04 <0E> 81 Blocked 0000 Off    0  DiagnosticESDI
 5 SWB-04 <0F> 81 Blocked 0000 Off    0  DiagnosticESDI
 6 SWB-04 <12> 81 Blocked 0000 Off    0  DiagnosticRAM
 7 SWB-04 <13> 81 Blocked 0000 Off    0  DiagnosticDrive
 8 SWB-04 <14> 81 Blocked 0000 Off    0  DiagnosticCTL
Results for SWB-04 category x on drive 81 All commands blocked (9 of 9)
 0 SWB-04 <05> 82 Blocked 0000 Off    0  FormatTrack
 1 SWB-04 <06> 82 Blocked 0000 Off    0  FormatBadSectors
 2 SWB-04 <07> 82 Blocked 0000 Off    0  FormatCyl
 3 SWB-04 <09> 82 Blocked 0000 Off    0  InitDriveParms
 4 SWB-04 <0E> 82 Blocked 0000 Off    0  DiagnosticESDI
 5 SWB-04 <0F> 82 Blocked 0000 Off    0  DiagnosticESDI
 6 SWB-04 <12> 82 Blocked 0000 Off    0  DiagnosticRAM
 7 SWB-04 <13> 82 Blocked 0000 Off    0  DiagnosticDrive
 8 SWB-04 <14> 82 Blocked 0000 Off    0  DiagnosticCTL
Results for SWB-04 category x on drive 82 All commands blocked (9 of 9)
 0 SWB-04 <05> 83 Blocked 0000 Off    0  FormatTrack
 1 SWB-04 <06> 83 Blocked 0000 Off    0  FormatBadSectors
 2 SWB-04 <07> 83 Blocked 0000 Off    0  FormatCyl
 3 SWB-04 <09> 83 Blocked 0000 Off    0  InitDriveParms
 4 SWB-04 <0E> 83 Blocked 0000 Off    0  DiagnosticESDI
 5 SWB-04 <0F> 83 Blocked 0000 Off    0  DiagnosticESDI
 6 SWB-04 <12> 83 Blocked 0000 Off    0  DiagnosticRAM
```

```
                 7 SWB-04 <13> 83 Blocked 0000 Off      0   DiagnosticDrive
                 8 SWB-04 <14> 83 Blocked 0000 Off      0   DiagnosticCTL
             Results for SWB-04 category x on drive 83 All commands blocked (9 of 9)
                 0 SWB-04 <05> 84 Blocked 0000 Off      0   FormatTrack
                 1 SWB-04 <06> 84 Blocked 0000 Off      0   FormatBadSectors
                 2 SWB-04 <07> 84 Blocked 0000 Off      0   FormatCyl
                 3 SWB-04 <09> 84 Blocked 0000 Off      0   InitDriveParms
                 4 SWB-04 <0E> 84 Blocked 0000 Off      0   DiagnosticESDI
                 5 SWB-04 <0F> 84 Blocked 0000 Off      0   DiagnosticESDI
                 6 SWB-04 <12> 84 Blocked 0000 Off      0   DiagnosticRAM
                 7 SWB-04 <13> 84 Blocked 0000 Off      0   DiagnosticDrive
                 8 SWB-04 <14> 84 Blocked 0000 Off      0   DiagnosticCTL
             Results for SWB-04 category x on drive 84 All commands blocked (9 of 9)
             Summary: 45 sent, 45 blocked, 0 not blocked
```

	Assertion	Expected Results	Actual Results
Results:	AM-02	All cmds to drive 80 blocked	All cmds to drive 80 blocked
	AM-02	All cmds to drive 81 blocked	All cmds to drive 81 blocked
	AM-02	All cmds to drive 82 blocked	All cmds to drive 82 blocked
	AM-02	All cmds to drive 83 blocked	All cmds to drive 83 blocked
	AM-02	All cmds to drive 84 blocked	All cmds to drive 84 blocked
	AM-07	Tool active message	Tool active message
	AM-08	5 drives identified	5 drives identified
	AM-09	Drive 80 is protected	Drive 80 is protected
	AM-09	Drive 81 is protected	Drive 81 is protected
	AM-09	Drive 82 is protected	Drive 82 is protected
	AM-09	Drive 83 is protected	Drive 83 is protected
	AM-09	Drive 84 is protected	Drive 84 is protected
	AM-10	45 Commands return success	45 Commands return success

Analysis:	SWB-04 Expected results achieved

Case SWB-05 HDL -- Int_13 Hard Disk Write Lock V0.8 021126 © RCMP 1993-2002

Case Summary:	SWB-05 Install two drives, configure return code to failure, protect all drives, execute miscellaneous commands.
Assertions Tested:	SWB-AM-03. If a drive is protected and a command from the miscellaneous category is issued for the protected drive then the tool shall block the command. SWB-AM-07. If the tool is executed then the tool shall issue a message indicating that the tool is active. SWB-AM-08. If the tool is executed then the tool shall issue a message indicating all drives accessible by the covered interfaces. SWB-AM-09. If the tool is executed then the tool shall issue a message indicating the protection status of each drive attached to a covered interface. SWB-AM-11. If the tool is configured to return fail on blocked commands and the tool blocks a command then the return code shall indicate unsuccessful command execution.
Tester Name:	JRL
Test Date:	Sun Aug 31 09:18:47 2003
Test PC:	Cadfael
Test Software:	SWBT 1.0
Hard Drives Used:	Drive 80, label F5 is an IBM-DTLA-307020 with 40188960 sectors Drive 81, label F6 is an IBM-DTLA-307020 with 40188960 sectors
Commands Executed:	Boot Test PC to (DOS 7.1) Windows 98 [Version 4.10.2222] tally13 hd18 01 test-hdl SWB-05 Cadfael JRL m F5 F6 Shutdown Test PC
Log File Highlights:	***** Monitor Execution ***** Monitor BIOS interrupt 13h (disk service) tally13 compiled on 07/29/03 at 07:33:17 @(#) Version 1.1 Created 07/29/03 at 07:28:05 Now (08/31/03 at 09:18:40) Going . . . TSR

```
***** Install HDL Log *****
HDL -- Int_13 Hard Disk Write Lock V0.8 021126 (c)RCMP 1993-2002
            ---- Royal Canadian Mounted Police ----
            UNAUTHORIZED  USE / DISTRIBUTION  PROHIBITED

            Licensee: US Dept. Commerce / NIST S/W Testing
            2  Hard-Disks reported by Int_13h
            Hard-Disk 0      Locked!
            Hard-Disk 1      Locked!
            Write Lock successfully installed.
***** Test Harness Log *****
CMD: A:\TEST-HDL.EXE SWB-05 Cadfael JRL m F5 F6
Case: SWB-05
Command set: Misc
Date: Sun Aug 31 09:18:47 2003

Version: @(#) test-hdl.cpp Version 1.1 Created 08/23/03 at 10:13:51
         @(#) wb-defs.h Version 1.2 Created 08/31/03 at 08:18:19
         Compiled on Aug 31 2003 at 08:10:54
Operator: JRL
Host: Cadfael
Number of drives 2, Drives: F5 F6
    Case  Cmd Drv Action  Stat Cry Count Cmd Name
  0 SWB-05 <16> 80 Blocked 0300 On       0 Undefined
        ...

        misc commands 17-FD results omitted

        see log files for full results

        ...

226 SWB-05 <FE> 80 Blocked 0300 On       0 Undefined
227 SWB-05 <FF> 80 Blocked 0300 On       0 Undefined
Results for SWB-05 category m on drive 80 All commands blocked (228 of
228)
  0 SWB-05 <16> 81 Blocked 0300 On       0 Undefined
        ...

        misc commands 17-FD results omitted

        see log files for full results

        ...

226 SWB-05 <FE> 81 Blocked 0300 On       0 Undefined
227 SWB-05 <FF> 81 Blocked 0300 On       0 Undefined
Results for SWB-05 category m on drive 81 All commands blocked (228 of
228)
Summary: 456 sent, 456 blocked, 0 not blocked
```

Results:

Assertion	Expected Results	Actual Results
AM-03	All cmds to drive 80 blocked	All cmds to drive 80 blocked
AM-03	All cmds to drive 81 blocked	All cmds to drive 81 blocked
AM-07	Tool active message	Tool active message
AM-08	2 drives identified	2 drives identified
AM-09	Drive 80 is protected	Drive 80 is protected
AM-09	Drive 81 is protected	Drive 81 is protected
AM-11	456 Commands return fail	456 Commands return fail

Analysis: SWB-05 Expected results achieved

Case SWB-06 HDL -- Int_13 Hard Disk Write Lock V0.8 021126 © RCMP 1993-2002

Case Summary:	SWB-06 Install one drive, configure return code to success, protect all drives, execute miscellaneous commands.
Assertions Tested:	SWB-AM-03. If a drive is protected and a command from the miscellaneous category is issued for the protected drive then the tool shall block the command.

	SWB-AM-07. If the tool is executed then the tool shall issue a message indicating that the tool is active. SWB-AM-08. If the tool is executed then the tool shall issue a message indicating all drives accessible by the covered interfaces. SWB-AM-09. If the tool is executed then the tool shall issue a message indicating the protection status of each drive attached to a covered interface. SWB-AM-10. If the tool is configured to return success on blocked commands and the tool blocks a command then the return code shall indicate successful command execution.
Tester Name:	JRL
Test Date:	Thu Aug 28 08:08:23 2003
Test PC:	AndWife
Test Software:	SWBT 1.0
Hard Drives Used:	Drive 80, label E4 is a QUANTUM ATLAS10K2-TY092J with 17938985 sectors
Commands Executed:	Boot Test PC to (DOS 7.1) Windows 98 [Version 4.10.2222] tally13 hdl8 S0 test-hdl SWB-06 AndWife JRL m E4 Shutdown Test PC

Log File Highlights:	***** Monitor Execution *****
	Monitor BIOS interrupt 13h (disk service)
	tally13 compiled on 07/29/03 at 07:33:17
	@(#) Version 1.1 Created 07/29/03 at 07:28:05
	Now (08/28/03 at 08:08:15) Going . . . TSR
	***** Install HDL Log *****
	HDL -- Int_13 Hard Disk Write Lock V0.8 021126 (c)RCMP 1993-2002
	    ---- Royal Canadian Mounted Police ----
	    UNAUTHORIZED USE / DISTRIBUTION PROHIBITED
	
	    Licensee: US Dept. Commerce / NIST S/W Testing
	    1 Hard-Disks reported by Int_13h
	    Hard-Disk 0 Locked!
	    Write Lock successfully installed.
	***** Test Harness Log *****
	CMD: A:\TEST-HDL.EXE SWB-06 AndWife JRL m E4
	Case: SWB-06
	Command set: Misc
	Date: Thu Aug 28 08:08:23 2003
	
	Version: @(#) test-hdl.cpp Version 1.1 Created 08/23/03 at 10:13:51
	    @(#) wb-defs.h Version 1.2 Created 08/31/03 at 08:18:19
	    Compiled on Aug 31 2003 at 08:10:54
	Operator: JRL
	Host: AndWife
	Number of drives 1, Drives: E4
	    Case Cmd Drv Action Stat Cry Count Cmd Name
	  0 SWB-06 <16> 80 Blocked 0000 Off 0 Undefined
	    ...
	
	    misc commands 17-FD results omitted
	
	    see log files for full results
	
	    ...
	
	226 SWB-06 <FE> 80 Blocked 0000 Off 0 Undefined
	227 SWB-06 <FF> 80 Blocked 0000 Off 0 Undefined
	Results for SWB-06 category m on drive 80 All commands blocked (228 of 228)
	Summary: 228 sent, 228 blocked, 0 not blocked

Results:	

Assertion	Expected Results	Actual Results
AM-03	All cmds to drive 80 blocked	All cmds to drive 80 blocked
AM-07	Tool active message	Tool active message
AM-08	1 drive identified	1 drive identified
AM-09	Drive 80 is protected	Drive 80 is protected
AM-10	228 Commands return success	228 Commands return success

Analysis:	SWB-06 Expected results achieved

Case SWB-07 HDL -- Int_13 Hard Disk Write Lock V0.8 021126 © RCMP 1993-2002	
Case Summary:	SWB-07 Install all drives, configure return code to failure, protect all drives, execute read commands.
Assertions Tested:	SWB-AM-04. If a drive is protected and a command from the read category is issued for the protected drive then the tool shall not block the command. SWB-AM-07. If the tool is executed then the tool shall issue a message indicating that the tool is active. SWB-AM-08. If the tool is executed then the tool shall issue a message indicating all drives accessible by the covered interfaces. SWB-AM-09. If the tool is executed then the tool shall issue a message indicating the protection status of each drive attached to a covered interface. SWB-AM-11. If the tool is configured to return fail on blocked commands and the tool blocks a command then the return code shall indicate unsuccessful command execution.
Tester Name:	JRL
Test Date:	Sun Aug 31 09:31:05 2003
Test PC:	Wimsey
Test Software:	SWBT 1.0
Hard Drives Used:	Drive 80, label 90 is a WDC WD300BB-00CAA0 with 58633344 sectors Drive 81, label 8A is a WDC WD200EB-00CSF0 with 39102336 sectors Drive 82, label E4 is a QUANTUM ATLAS10K2-TY092J with 17938985 sectors Drive 83, label 2B is a Quantum QM39100TD-SCA Drive with 17783249 sectors
Commands Executed:	Boot Test PC to (DOS 7.1) Windows 98 [Version 4.10.2222] tally13 hdl8 0123 test-hdl SWB-07 Wimsey JRL r 90 8A E4 2B Shutdown Test PC

Log File Highlights:	***** Monitor Execution *****
	Monitor BIOS interrupt 13h (disk service)
	tally13 compiled on 07/29/03 at 07:33:17
	@(#) Version 1.1 Created 07/29/03 at 07:28:05
	Now (08/31/03 at 09:31:02) Going . . . TSR
	***** Install HDL Log *****
	HDL -- Int_13 Hard Disk Write Lock V0.8 021126 (c)RCMP 1993-2002
	    ---- Royal Canadian Mounted Police ----
	    UNAUTHORIZED USE / DISTRIBUTION PROHIBITED
	
	    Licensee: US Dept. Commerce / NIST S/W Testing
	    4 Hard-Disks reported by Int_13h
	    Hard-Disk 0 Locked!
	    Hard-Disk 1 Locked!
	    Hard-Disk 2 Locked!
	    Hard-Disk 3 Locked!
	    Write Lock successfully installed.
	***** Test Harness Log *****
	CMD: A:\TEST-HDL.EXE SWB-07 Wimsey JRL r 90 8A E4 2B
	Case: SWB-07
	Command set: Read
	Date: Sun Aug 31 09:31:05 2003
	
	Version: @(#) test-hdl.cpp Version 1.1 Created 08/23/03 at 10:13:51
	    @(#) wb-defs.h Version 1.2 Created 08/31/03 at 08:18:19
	    Compiled on Aug 31 2003 at 08:10:54
	Operator: JRL
	Host: Wimsey
	Number of drives 4, Drives: 90 8A E4 2B
	    Case Cmd Drv Action Stat Cry Count Cmd Name
	 0 SWB-07 <02> 80 Allowed 0000 Off 1 ReadSectors
	 1 SWB-07 <0A> 80 Allowed 0000 Off 1 ReadLong
	 2 SWB-07 <42> 80 Allowed 0000 Off 1 ExtRead
	Results for SWB-07 category r on drive 80 No commands blocked (0 of 3)
	 0 SWB-07 <02> 81 Allowed 0000 Off 1 ReadSectors
	 1 SWB-07 <0A> 81 Allowed 0000 Off 1 ReadLong
	 2 SWB-07 <42> 81 Allowed 0000 Off 1 ExtRead
	Results for SWB-07 category r on drive 81 No commands blocked (0 of 3)
	 0 SWB-07 <02> 82 Allowed 0000 Off 1 ReadSectors

Case SWB-07 HDL -- Int_13 Hard Disk Write Lock V0.8 021126 © RCMP 1993-2002	
	1 SWB-07 <0A> 82 Allowed 0000 Off 1 ReadLong 2 SWB-07 <42> 82 Allowed 0000 Off 1 ExtRead Results for SWB-07 category r on drive 82 No commands blocked (0 of 3) 0 SWB-07 <02> 83 Allowed 0000 Off 1 ReadSectors 1 SWB-07 <0A> 83 Allowed 0000 Off 1 ReadLong 2 SWB-07 <42> 83 Allowed 0000 Off 1 ExtRead Results for SWB-07 category r on drive 83 No commands blocked (0 of 3) Summary: 12 sent, 0 blocked, 12 not blocked
Results:	

Assertion	Expected Results	Actual Results
AM-04	No cmds to drive 80 blocked	No cmds to drive 80 blocked
AM-04	No cmds to drive 81 blocked	No cmds to drive 81 blocked
AM-04	No cmds to drive 82 blocked	No cmds to drive 82 blocked
AM-04	No cmds to drive 83 blocked	No cmds to drive 83 blocked
AM-07	Tool active message	Tool active message
AM-08	4 drives identified	4 drives identified
AM-09	Drive 80 is protected	Drive 80 is protected
AM-09	Drive 81 is protected	Drive 81 is protected
AM-09	Drive 82 is protected	Drive 82 is protected
AM-09	Drive 83 is protected	Drive 83 is protected
AM-11	0 Commands return fail	0 Commands return fail

Analysis:	SWB-07 Expected results achieved

Case SWB-08 HDL -- Int_13 Hard Disk Write Lock V0.8 021126 © RCMP 1993-2002	
Case Summary:	SWB-08 Install two drives, configure return code to success, protect all drives, execute read commands.
Assertions Tested:	SWB-AM-04. If a drive is protected and a command from the read category is issued for the protected drive then the tool shall not block the command. SWB-AM-07. If the tool is executed then the tool shall issue a message indicating that the tool is active. SWB-AM-08. If the tool is executed then the tool shall issue a message indicating all drives accessible by the covered interfaces. SWB-AM-09. If the tool is executed then the tool shall issue a message indicating the protection status of each drive attached to a covered interface. SWB-AM-10. If the tool is configured to return success on blocked commands and the tool blocks a command then the return code shall indicate successful command execution.
Tester Name:	JRL
Test Date:	Sun Aug 31 08:06:45 2003
Test PC:	Rumpole
Test Software:	SWBT 1.0
Hard Drives Used:	Drive 80, label 2B is a Quantum QM39100TD-SCA Drive with 17783249 sectors Drive 81, label 1F is a Quantum ATLAS10K3_18_SCA Drive with 35916548 sectors
Commands Executed:	Boot Test PC to (DOS 7.1) Windows 98 [Version 4.10.2222] tally13 hdl8 S01 test-hdl SWB-08 Rumpole JRL r 2B 1F Shutdown Test PC

Log File Highlights:	***** Monitor Execution *****
	Monitor BIOS interrupt 13h (disk service)
	tally13 compiled on 07/29/03 at 07:33:17
	@(#) Version 1.1 Created 07/29/03 at 07:28:05
	Now (08/31/03 at 08:06:42) Going . . . TSR
	***** Install HDL Log *****
	HDL -- Int_13 Hard Disk Write Lock V0.8 021126 (c)RCMP 1993-2002
	     ---- Royal Canadian Mounted Police ----
	     UNAUTHORIZED USE / DISTRIBUTION PROHIBITED
	
	     Licensee: US Dept. Commerce / NIST S/W Testing
	     2 Hard-Disks reported by Int_13h
	     Hard-Disk 0 Locked!
	     Hard-Disk 1 Locked!
	     Write Lock successfully installed.
	***** Test Harness Log *****

	CMD: A:\TEST-HDL.EXE SWB-08 Rumpole JRL r 2B 1F
	Case: SWB-08
	Command set: Read
	Date: Sun Aug 31 08:06:45 2003
	
	Version: @(#) test-hdl.cpp Version 1.1 Created 08/23/03 at 10:13:51
	      @(#) wb-defs.h Version 1.2 Created 08/31/03 at 08:18:19
	        Compiled on Aug 31 2003 at 08:10:54
	Operator: JRL
	Host: Rumpole
	Number of drives 2, Drives: 2B 1F
	     Case Cmd Drv Action Stat Cry Count Cmd Name
	  0 SWB-08 <02> 80 Allowed 0000 Off 1 ReadSectors
	  1 SWB-08 <0A> 80 Allowed 0000 Off 1 ReadLong
	  2 SWB-08 <42> 80 Allowed 0000 Off 1 ExtRead
	Results for SWB-08 category r on drive 80 No commands blocked (0 of 3)
	  0 SWB-08 <02> 81 Allowed 0000 Off 1 ReadSectors
	  1 SWB-08 <0A> 81 Allowed 0000 Off 1 ReadLong
	  2 SWB-08 <42> 81 Allowed 0000 Off 1 ExtRead
	Results for SWB-08 category r on drive 81 No commands blocked (0 of 3)
	Summary: 6 sent, 0 blocked, 6 not blocked

Results:	

Assertion	Expected Results	Actual Results
AM-04	No cmds to drive 80 blocked	No cmds to drive 80 blocked
AM-04	No cmds to drive 81 blocked	No cmds to drive 81 blocked
AM-07	Tool active message	Tool active message
AM-08	2 drives identified	2 drives identified
AM-09	Drive 80 is protected	Drive 80 is protected
AM-09	Drive 81 is protected	Drive 81 is protected
AM-10	0 Commands return success	0 Commands return success

Analysis:	SWB-08 Expected results achieved

Case Summary:	SWB-09 Install one drive, configure return code to failure, protect all drives, execute information commands.
Assertions Tested:	SWB-AM-06. If a drive is protected and a command from the information category is issued for the protected drive then the tool shall not block the command. SWB-AM-07. If the tool is executed then the tool shall issue a message indicating that the tool is active. SWB-AM-08. If the tool is executed then the tool shall issue a message indicating all drives accessible by the covered interfaces. SWB-AM-09. If the tool is executed then the tool shall issue a message indicating the protection status of each drive attached to a covered interface. SWB-AM-11. If the tool is configured to return fail on blocked commands and the tool blocks a command then the return code shall indicate unsuccessful command execution.
Tester Name:	JRL
Test Date:	Sun Aug 31 09:09:07 2003
Test PC:	McMloud
Test Software:	SWBT 1.0
Hard Drives Used:	Drive 80, label 8A is a WDC WD200EB-00CSF0 with 39102336 sectors
Commands Executed:	Boot Test PC to (DOS 7.1) Windows 98 [Version 4.10.2222] tally13 hdl8 0 test-hdl SWB-09 McMloud JRL i 8A Shutdown Test PC

Log File Highlights:	***** Monitor Execution *****
	Monitor BIOS interrupt 13h (disk service)
	tally13 compiled on 07/29/03 at 07:33:17
	@(#) Version 1.1 Created 07/29/03 at 07:28:05
	Now (08/31/03 at 09:09:00) Going . . . TSR
	***** Install HDL Log *****
	HDL -- Int_13 Hard Disk Write Lock V0.8 021126 (c)RCMP 1993-2002
	      ---- Royal Canadian Mounted Police ----
	      UNAUTHORIZED USE / DISTRIBUTION PROHIBITED

Case SWB-09 HDL -- Int_13 Hard Disk Write Lock V0.8 021126 © RCMP 1993-2002

```
                    Licensee: US Dept. Commerce / NIST S/W Testing
                    1  Hard-Disks reported by Int_13h
                    Hard-Disk 0     Locked!
                    Write Lock successfully installed.
             ***** Test Harness Log *****
             CMD: A:\TEST-HDL.EXE SWB-09 McMloud JRL i 8A
             Case: SWB-09
             Command set: Information
             Date: Sun Aug 31 09:09:07 2003

             Version: @(#) test-hdl.cpp Version 1.1 Created 08/23/03 at 10:13:51
                      @(#) wb-defs.h Version 1.2 Created 08/31/03 at 08:18:19
                      Compiled on Aug 31 2003 at 08:10:54
             Operator: JRL
             Host: McMloud
             Number of drives 1, Drives: 8A
                  Case  Cmd Drv Action  Stat Cry Count Cmd Name
              0 SWB-09 <01> 80 Allowed 0000 Off    1  GetLastStatus
              1 SWB-09 <04> 80 Allowed 0000 Off    1  VerifySectors
              2 SWB-09 <08> 80 Allowed 0000 Off    1  ReadDriveParms
              3 SWB-09 <10> 80 Allowed 0000 Off    1  TestDriveReady
              4 SWB-09 <15> 80 Allowed 0000 Off    1  ReadDriveType
              5 SWB-09 <41> 80 Allowed 0000 Off    1  CheckForExtensions
              6 SWB-09 <44> 80 Allowed 0000 Off    1  VerifySectors
              7 SWB-09 <48> 80 Allowed 0000 Off    1  GetDriveParms
             Results for SWB-09 category i on drive 80 No commands blocked (0 of 8)
             Summary: 8 sent, 0 blocked, 8 not blocked
```

Results:			
	Assertion	**Expected Results**	**Actual Results**
	AM-06	All cmds to drive 80 blocked	All cmds to drive 80 blocked
	AM-07	Tool active message	Tool active message
	AM-08	1 drive identified	1 drive identified
	AM-09	Drive 80 is protected	Drive 80 is protected
	AM-11	0 Commands return fail	0 Commands return fail

Analysis:	SWB-09 Expected results achieved

Case SWB-10 HDL -- Int_13 Hard Disk Write Lock V0.8 021126 © RCMP 1993-2002

Case Summary:	SWB-10 Install all drives, configure return code to success, protect all drives, execute information commands.
Assertions Tested:	SWB-AM-06. If a drive is protected and a command from the information category is issued for the protected drive then the tool shall not block the command. SWB-AM-07. If the tool is executed then the tool shall issue a message indicating that the tool is active. SWB-AM-08. If the tool is executed then the tool shall issue a message indicating all drives accessible by the covered interfaces. SWB-AM-09. If the tool is executed then the tool shall issue a message indicating the protection status of each drive attached to a covered interface. SWB-AM-10. If the tool is configured to return success on blocked commands and the tool blocks a command then the return code shall indicate successful command execution.
Tester Name:	JRL
Test Date:	Sun Aug 31 09:33:02 2003
Test PC:	HecRamsey
Test Software:	SWBT 1.0
Hard Drives Used:	Drive 80, label F5 is an IBM-DTLA-307020 with 40188960 sectors Drive 81, label 64 is a WDC WD64AA with 12594960 sectors Drive 82, label 6F is a Maxtor 6Y060L0 with 120103200 sectors Drive 83, label E3 is a QUANTUM ATLAS10K2-TY092J with 17938985 sectors Drive 84, label 1F is a Quantum ATLAS10K3_18_SCA Drive with 35916548 sectors
Commands Executed:	Boot Test PC to (DOS 7.1) Windows 98 [Version 4.10.2222] tally13 hdl8 S01234 test-hdl SWB-10 HecRamsey JRL i F5 64 6F E3 1F

	Shutdown Test PC
| Log File Highlights: | ```
***** Monitor Execution *****
Monitor BIOS interrupt 13h (disk service)
tally13  compiled on 07/29/03 at 07:33:17
@(#) Version 1.1 Created 07/29/03 at 07:28:05
Now (08/31/03 at 09:32:55) Going . . .   TSR
***** Install HDL Log *****
HDL -- Int_13 Hard Disk Write Lock V0.8 021126 (c)RCMP 1993-2002
         ---- Royal  Canadian  Mounted  Police  ----
         UNAUTHORIZED  USE / DISTRIBUTION  PROHIBITED

         Licensee: US Dept. Commerce / NIST S/W Testing
         5  Hard-Disks reported by Int_13h
         Hard-Disk 0     Locked!
         Hard-Disk 1     Locked!
         Hard-Disk 2     Locked!
         Hard-Disk 3     Locked!
         Hard-Disk 4     Locked!
         Write Lock successfully installed.
***** Test Harness Log *****
CMD: A:\TEST-HDL.EXE SWB-10 HecRamsey JRL i F5 64 6F E3 1F
Case: SWB-10
Command set: Information
Date: Sun Aug 31 09:33:02 2003

Version: @(#) test-hdl.cpp Version 1.1 Created 08/23/03 at 10:13:51
         @(#) wb-defs.h Version 1.2 Created 08/31/03 at 08:18:19
         Compiled on Aug 31 2003 at 08:10:54
Operator: JRL
Host: HecRamsey
Number of drives 5, Drives: F5 64 6F E3 1F
     Case  Cmd Drv Action  Stat Cry Count Cmd Name
 0 SWB-10 <01> 80 Allowed 0000 Off    1  GetLastStatus
 1 SWB-10 <04> 80 Allowed 0000 Off    1  VerifySectors
 2 SWB-10 <08> 80 Allowed 0000 Off    1  ReadDriveParms
 3 SWB-10 <10> 80 Allowed 0000 Off    1  TestDriveReady
 4 SWB-10 <15> 80 Allowed 0000 Off    1  ReadDriveType
 5 SWB-10 <41> 80 Allowed 0000 Off    1  CheckForExtensions
 6 SWB-10 <44> 80 Allowed 0000 Off    1  VerifySectors
 7 SWB-10 <48> 80 Allowed 0000 Off    1  GetDriveParms
Results for SWB-10 category i on drive 80 No commands blocked (0 of 8)
 0 SWB-10 <01> 81 Allowed 0000 Off    1  GetLastStatus
 1 SWB-10 <04> 81 Allowed 0000 Off    1  VerifySectors
 2 SWB-10 <08> 81 Allowed 0000 Off    1  ReadDriveParms
 3 SWB-10 <10> 81 Allowed 0000 Off    1  TestDriveReady
 4 SWB-10 <15> 81 Allowed 0000 Off    1  ReadDriveType
 5 SWB-10 <41> 81 Allowed 0000 Off    1  CheckForExtensions
 6 SWB-10 <44> 81 Allowed 0000 Off    1  VerifySectors
 7 SWB-10 <48> 81 Allowed 0000 Off    1  GetDriveParms
Results for SWB-10 category i on drive 81 No commands blocked (0 of 8)
 0 SWB-10 <01> 82 Allowed 0000 Off    1  GetLastStatus
 1 SWB-10 <04> 82 Allowed 0000 Off    1  VerifySectors
 2 SWB-10 <08> 82 Allowed 0000 Off    1  ReadDriveParms
 3 SWB-10 <10> 82 Allowed 0000 Off    1  TestDriveReady
 4 SWB-10 <15> 82 Allowed 0000 Off    1  ReadDriveType
 5 SWB-10 <41> 82 Allowed 0000 Off    1  CheckForExtensions
 6 SWB-10 <44> 82 Allowed 0000 Off    1  VerifySectors
 7 SWB-10 <48> 82 Allowed 0000 Off    1  GetDriveParms
Results for SWB-10 category i on drive 82 No commands blocked (0 of 8)
 0 SWB-10 <01> 83 Allowed 0000 Off    1  GetLastStatus
 1 SWB-10 <04> 83 Allowed 0000 Off    1  VerifySectors
 2 SWB-10 <08> 83 Allowed 0000 Off    1  ReadDriveParms
 3 SWB-10 <10> 83 Allowed 0000 Off    1  TestDriveReady
 4 SWB-10 <15> 83 Allowed 0000 Off    1  ReadDriveType
 5 SWB-10 <41> 83 Allowed 0000 Off    1  CheckForExtensions
 6 SWB-10 <44> 83 Allowed 0000 Off    1  VerifySectors
 7 SWB-10 <48> 83 Allowed 0000 Off    1  GetDriveParms
Results for SWB-10 category i on drive 83 No commands blocked (0 of 8)
 0 SWB-10 <01> 84 Allowed 0000 Off    1  GetLastStatus
 1 SWB-10 <04> 84 Allowed 0000 Off    1  VerifySectors
 2 SWB-10 <08> 84 Allowed 0000 Off    1  ReadDriveParms
 3 SWB-10 <10> 84 Allowed 0000 Off    1  TestDriveReady
 4 SWB-10 <15> 84 Allowed 0000 Off    1  ReadDriveType
``` |
```

```
          5 SWB-10 <41> 84 Allowed 0000 Off     1  CheckForExtensions
          6 SWB-10 <44> 84 Allowed 0000 Off     1  VerifySectors
          7 SWB-10 <48> 84 Allowed 0000 Off     1  GetDriveParms
        Results for SWB-10 category i on drive 84 No commands blocked (0 of 8)
        Summary: 40 sent, 0 blocked, 40 not blocked
```

Results:		

Assertion	Expected Results	Actual Results
AM-06	No cmds to drive 80 blocked	No cmds to drive 80 blocked
AM-06	No cmds to drive 81 blocked	No cmds to drive 81 blocked
AM-06	No cmds to drive 82 blocked	No cmds to drive 82 blocked
AM-06	No cmds to drive 83 blocked	No cmds to drive 83 blocked
AM-06	No cmds to drive 84 blocked	No cmds to drive 84 blocked
AM-07	Tool active message	Tool active message
AM-08	5 drives identified	5 drives identified
AM-09	Drive 80 is protected	Drive 80 is protected
AM-09	Drive 81 is protected	Drive 81 is protected
AM-09	Drive 82 is protected	Drive 82 is protected
AM-09	Drive 83 is protected	Drive 83 is protected
AM-09	Drive 84 is protected	Drive 84 is protected
AM-10	0 Commands return success	0 Commands return success

Analysis:	SWB-10 Expected results achieved

Case Summary:	SWB-11 Install two drives, configure return code to failure, protect all drives, execute control commands.
Assertions Tested:	SWB-AM-05. If a drive is protected and a command from the control category is issued for the protected drive then the tool shall not block the command. SWB-AM-07. If the tool is executed then the tool shall issue a message indicating that the tool is active. SWB-AM-08. If the tool is executed then the tool shall issue a message indicating all drives accessible by the covered interfaces. SWB-AM-09. If the tool is executed then the tool shall issue a message indicating the protection status of each drive attached to a covered interface. SWB-AM-11. If the tool is configured to return fail on blocked commands and the tool blocks a command then the return code shall indicate unsuccessful command execution.
Tester Name:	JRL
Test Date:	Sun Aug 31 08:09:56 2003
Test PC:	Rumpole
Test Software:	SWBT 1.0
Hard Drives Used:	Drive 80, label 2B is a Quantum QM39100TD-SCA Drive with 17783249 sectors Drive 81, label 1F is a Quantum ATLAS10K3_18_SCA Drive with 35916548 sectors
Commands Executed:	Boot Test PC to (DOS 7.1) Windows 98 [Version 4.10.2222] tally13 hdl8 01 test-hdl SWB-11 Rumpole JRL c 2B 1F Shutdown Test PC

Log File Highlights:	***** Monitor Execution *****
	Monitor BIOS interrupt 13h (disk service)
	tally13 compiled on 07/29/03 at 07:33:17
	@(#) Version 1.1 Created 07/29/03 at 07:28:05
	Now (08/31/03 at 08:09:53) Going . . . TSR
	***** Install HDL Log *****
	HDL -- Int_13 Hard Disk Write Lock V0.8 021126 (c)RCMP 1993-2002
	    ---- Royal Canadian Mounted Police ----
	    UNAUTHORIZED USE / DISTRIBUTION PROHIBITED
	
	    Licensee: US Dept. Commerce / NIST S/W Testing
	    2 Hard-Disks reported by Int_13h
	    Hard-Disk 0 Locked!
	    Hard-Disk 1 Locked!
	    Write Lock successfully installed.
	***** Test Harness Log *****
	CMD: A:\TEST-HDL.EXE SWB-11 Rumpole JRL c 2B 1F

	Case: SWB-11
	Command set: Control
	Date: Sun Aug 31 08:09:56 2003
	
	Version: @(#) test-hdl.cpp Version 1.1 Created 08/23/03 at 10:13:51
	      @(#) wb-defs.h Version 1.2 Created 08/31/03 at 08:18:19
	        Compiled on Aug 31 2003 at 08:10:54
	Operator: JRL
	Host: Rumpole
	Number of drives 2, Drives: 2B 1F

```
        Case  Cmd Drv Action  Stat Cry Count Cmd Name
   0 SWB-11 <00> 80 Allowed 0000 Off    1   Reset
   1 SWB-11 <0C> 80 Allowed 0000 Off    1   SeekDrive
   2 SWB-11 <0D> 80 Allowed 0000 Off    1   AltReset
   3 SWB-11 <11> 80 Blocked 0300 On     0   Recalibrate
   4 SWB-11 <47> 80 Blocked 0300 On     0   ExtendedSeek
Results for SWB-11 category c on drive 80 Not all commands blocked (2
of 5)
   0 SWB-11 <00> 81 Allowed 0000 Off    1   Reset
   1 SWB-11 <0C> 81 Allowed 0000 Off    1   SeekDrive
   2 SWB-11 <0D> 81 Allowed 0000 Off    1   AltReset
   3 SWB-11 <11> 81 Blocked 0300 On     0   Recalibrate
   4 SWB-11 <47> 81 Blocked 0300 On     0   ExtendedSeek
Results for SWB-11 category c on drive 81 Not all commands blocked (2
of 5)
Summary: 10 sent, 4 blocked, 6 not blocked
```

Results:			
	Assertion	**Expected Results**	**Actual Results**
	AM-05	No cmds to drive 80 blocked	Not all cmds to drive 80 blocked
	AM-05	No cmds to drive 81 blocked	Not all cmds to drive 81 blocked
	AM-07	Tool active message	Tool active message
	AM-08	2 drives identified	2 drives identified
	AM-09	Drive 80 is protected	Drive 80 is protected
	AM-09	Drive 81 is protected	Drive 81 is protected
	AM-11	4 Commands return fail	4 Commands return fail

Analysis:	SWB-11 Expected results not achieved for assertions: AM-05

Case Summary:	SWB-12 Install one drive, configure return code to success, protect all drives, execute control commands.
Assertions Tested:	SWB-AM-05. If a drive is protected and a command from the control category is issued for the protected drive then the tool shall not block the command. SWB-AM-07. If the tool is executed then the tool shall issue a message indicating that the tool is active. SWB-AM-08. If the tool is executed then the tool shall issue a message indicating all drives accessible by the covered interfaces. SWB-AM-09. If the tool is executed then the tool shall issue a message indicating the protection status of each drive attached to a covered interface. SWB-AM-10. If the tool is configured to return success on blocked commands and the tool blocks a command then the return code shall indicate successful command execution.
Tester Name:	JRL
Test Date:	Thu Aug 28 08:16:26 2003
Test PC:	AndWife
Test Software:	SWBT 1.0
Hard Drives Used:	Drive 80, label E4 is a QUANTUM ATLAS10K2-TY092J with 17938985 sectors
Commands Executed:	Boot Test PC to (DOS 7.1) Windows 98 [Version 4.10.2222] tally13 hdl8 S0 test-hdl SWB-12 AndWife JRL c E4 Shutdown Test PC
Log File Highlights:	***** Monitor Execution ***** Monitor BIOS interrupt 13h (disk service)

```
tally13  compiled on 07/29/03 at 07:33:17
@(#) Version 1.1 Created 07/29/03 at 07:28:05
Now (08/28/03 at 08:16:19) Going . . .  TSR
***** Install HDL Log *****
HDL -- Int_13 Hard Disk Write Lock V0.8 021126 (c)RCMP 1993-2002
       ----  Royal  Canadian  Mounted  Police  ----
       UNAUTHORIZED  USE / DISTRIBUTION  PROHIBITED

       Licensee: US Dept. Commerce / NIST S/W Testing
       1  Hard-Disks reported by Int_13h
       Hard-Disk 0     Locked!
       Write Lock successfully installed.
***** Test Harness Log *****
CMD: A:\TEST-HDL.EXE SWB-12 AndWife JRL c E4
Case: SWB-12
Command set: Control
Date: Thu Aug 28 08:16:26 2003

Version: @(#) test-hdl.cpp Version 1.1 Created 08/23/03 at 10:13:51
         @(#) wb-defs.h Version 1.2 Created 08/31/03 at 08:18:19
         Compiled on Aug 31 2003 at 08:10:54
Operator: JRL
Host: AndWife
Number of drives 1, Drives: E4
     Case  Cmd Drv Action  Stat Cry Count Cmd Name
  0 SWB-12 <00> 80 Allowed 0000 Off      1 Reset
  1 SWB-12 <0C> 80 Allowed 0000 Off      1 SeekDrive
  2 SWB-12 <0D> 80 Allowed 0000 Off      1 AltReset
  3 SWB-12 <11> 80 Blocked 0000 Off      0 Recalibrate
  4 SWB-12 <47> 80 Blocked 0000 Off      0 ExtendedSeek
Results for SWB-12 category c on drive 80 Not all commands blocked (2
of 5)
Summary: 5 sent, 2 blocked, 3 not blocked
```

Results:			
	Assertion	**Expected Results**	**Actual Results**
	AM-05	No cmds to drive 80 blocked	Not all cmds to drive 80 blocked
	AM-07	Tool active message	Tool active message
	AM-08	1 drive identified	1 drive identified
	AM-09	Drive 80 is protected	Drive 80 is protected
	AM-10	2 Commands return success	2 Commands return success
Analysis:	SWB-12 Expected results not achieved for assertions: AM-05		

Case Summary:	SWB-13 Install all drives, configure return code to failure, protect with pattern odd, execute write commands.
Assertions Tested:	SWB-AM-07. If the tool is executed then the tool shall issue a message indicating that the tool is active.
	SWB-AM-08. If the tool is executed then the tool shall issue a message indicating all drives accessible by the covered interfaces.
	SWB-AM-09. If the tool is executed then the tool shall issue a message indicating the protection status of each drive attached to a covered interface.
	SWB-AM-11. If the tool is configured to return fail on blocked commands and the tool blocks a command then the return code shall indicate unsuccessful command execution.
	SWB-AO-01. If a subset of all covered drives is specified for protection, then commands from the write category shall be blocked for drives in the selected subset.
	SWB-AO-07. If a subset of all covered drives is specified for protection, then no commands from any category shall be blocked for drives not in the selected subset.
Tester Name:	JRL
Test Date:	Sun Aug 31 09:34:13 2003
Test PC:	Wimsey
Test Software:	SWBT 1.0
Hard Drives Used:	Drive 80, label 90 is a WDC WD300BB-00CAA0 with 58633344 sectors
	Drive 81, label 8A is a WDC WD200EB-00CSF0 with 39102336 sectors

	Drive 82, label E4 is a QUANTUM ATLAS10K2-TY092J with 17938985 sectors Drive 83, label 2B is a Quantum QM39100TD-SCA Drive with 17783249 sectors
Commands Executed:	Boot Test PC to (DOS 7.1) Windows 98 [Version 4.10.2222] tally13 hdl8 13 test-hdl SWB-13 Wimsey JRL w 90 8A E4 2B Shutdown Test PC

Log File Highlights:	***** Monitor Execution *****
	Monitor BIOS interrupt 13h (disk service)
	tally13 compiled on 07/29/03 at 07:33:17
	@(#) Version 1.1 Created 07/29/03 at 07:28:05
	Now (08/31/03 at 09:34:10) Going . . . TSR
	***** Install HDL Log *****
	HDL -- Int_13 Hard Disk Write Lock V0.8 021126 (c)RCMP 1993-2002
	    ---- Royal Canadian Mounted Police ----
	    UNAUTHORIZED USE / DISTRIBUTION PROHIBITED
	
	    Licensee: US Dept. Commerce / NIST S/W Testing
	    4 Hard-Disks reported by Int_13h
	    Hard-Disk 0 Not Locked!
	    Hard-Disk 1 Locked!
	    Hard-Disk 2 Not Locked!
	    Hard-Disk 3 Locked!
	    Write Lock successfully installed.
	***** Test Harness Log *****
	CMD: A:\TEST-HDL.EXE SWB-13 Wimsey JRL w 90 8A E4 2B
	Case: SWB-13
	Command set: Write
	Date: Sun Aug 31 09:34:13 2003
	
	Version: @(#) test-hdl.cpp Version 1.1 Created 08/23/03 at 10:13:51
	    @(#) wb-defs.h Version 1.2 Created 08/31/03 at 08:18:19
	    Compiled on Aug 31 2003 at 08:10:54
	Operator: JRL
	Host: Wimsey
	Number of drives 4, Drives: 90 8A E4 2B
	    Case Cmd Drv Action Stat Cry Count Cmd Name
	 0 SWB-13 <03> 80 Allowed 0000 Off 1 WriteSectors
	 1 SWB-13 <0B> 80 Allowed 0000 Off 1 WriteLong
	 2 SWB-13 <43> 80 Allowed 0000 Off 1 ExtWrite
	Results for SWB-13 category w on drive 80 No commands blocked (0 of 3)
	 0 SWB-13 <03> 81 Blocked 0300 On 0 WriteSectors
	 1 SWB-13 <0B> 81 Blocked 0300 On 0 WriteLong
	 2 SWB-13 <43> 81 Blocked 0300 On 0 ExtWrite
	Results for SWB-13 category w on drive 81 All commands blocked (3 of 3)
	 0 SWB-13 <03> 82 Allowed 0000 Off 1 WriteSectors
	 1 SWB-13 <0B> 82 Allowed 0000 Off 1 WriteLong
	 2 SWB-13 <43> 82 Allowed 0000 Off 1 ExtWrite
	Results for SWB-13 category w on drive 82 No commands blocked (0 of 3)
	 0 SWB-13 <03> 83 Blocked 0300 On 0 WriteSectors
	 1 SWB-13 <0B> 83 Blocked 0300 On 0 WriteLong
	 2 SWB-13 <43> 83 Blocked 0300 On 0 ExtWrite
	Results for SWB-13 category w on drive 83 All commands blocked (3 of 3)
	Summary: 12 sent, 6 blocked, 6 not blocked

Results:	

Assertion	Expected Results	Actual Results
AM-07	Tool active message	Tool active message
AM-08	4 drives identified	4 drives identified
AM-09	Drive 80 is unprotected	Drive 80 is unprotected
AM-09	Drive 81 is protected	Drive 81 is protected
AM-09	Drive 82 is unprotected	Drive 82 is unprotected
AM-09	Drive 83 is protected	Drive 83 is protected
AM-11	6 Commands return fail	6 Commands return fail
AO-01	All cmds to drive 81 blocked	All cmds to drive 81 blocked
AO-01	All cmds to drive 83 blocked	All cmds to drive 83 blocked
AO-07	No cmds to drive 80 blocked	No cmds to drive 80 blocked
AO-07	No cmds to drive 82 blocked	No cmds to drive 82 blocked

Analysis:	SWB-13 Expected results achieved

Case SWB-14 HDL -- Int_13 Hard Disk Write Lock V0.8 021126 © RCMP 1993-2002	
Case Summary:	SWB-14 Install all drives, configure return code to success, protect with pattern low, execute write commands.
Assertions Tested:	SWB-AM-07. If the tool is executed then the tool shall issue a message indicating that the tool is active. SWB-AM-08. If the tool is executed then the tool shall issue a message indicating all drives accessible by the covered interfaces. SWB-AM-09. If the tool is executed then the tool shall issue a message indicating the protection status of each drive attached to a covered interface. SWB-AM-10. If the tool is configured to return success on blocked commands and the tool blocks a command then the return code shall indicate successful command execution. SWB-AO-01. If a subset of all covered drives is specified for protection, then commands from the write category shall be blocked for drives in the selected subset. SWB-AO-07. If a subset of all covered drives is specified for protection, then no commands from any category shall be blocked for drives not in the selected subset.
Tester Name:	JRL
Test Date:	Sun Aug 31 09:35:58 2003
Test PC:	HecRamsey
Test Software:	SWBT 1.0
Hard Drives Used:	Drive 80, label F5 is an IBM-DTLA-307020 with 40188960 sectors Drive 81, label 64 is a WDC WD64AA with 12594960 sectors Drive 82, label 6F is a Maxtor 6Y060L0 with 120103200 sectors Drive 83, label E3 is a QUANTUM ATLAS10K2-TY092J with 17938985 sectors Drive 84, label 1F is a Quantum ATLAS10K3_18_SCA Drive with 35916548 sectors
Commands Executed:	Boot Test PC to (DOS 7.1) Windows 98 [Version 4.10.2222] tally13 hdl8 S01 test-hdl SWB-14 HecRamsey JRL w F5 64 6F E3 1F Shutdown Test PC

Log File Highlights:	***** Monitor Execution *****
	Monitor BIOS interrupt 13h (disk service)
	tally13 compiled on 07/29/03 at 07:33:17
	@(#) Version 1.1 Created 07/29/03 at 07:28:05
	Now (08/31/03 at 09:35:51) Going . . . TSR
	***** Install HDL Log *****
	HDL -- Int_13 Hard Disk Write Lock V0.8 021126 (c)RCMP 1993-2002
	    ---- Royal Canadian Mounted Police ----
	    UNAUTHORIZED USE / DISTRIBUTION PROHIBITED
	
	    Licensee: US Dept. Commerce / NIST S/W Testing
	    5 Hard-Disks reported by Int_13h
	    Hard-Disk 0 Locked!
	    Hard-Disk 1 Locked!
	    Hard-Disk 2 Not Locked!
	    Hard-Disk 3 Not Locked!
	    Hard-Disk 4 Not Locked!
	    Write Lock successfully installed.
	***** Test Harness Log *****
	CMD: A:\TEST-HDL.EXE SWB-14 HecRamsey JRL w F5 64 6F E3 1F
	Case: SWB-14
	Command set: Write
	Date: Sun Aug 31 09:35:58 2003
	
	Version: @(#) test-hdl.cpp Version 1.1 Created 08/23/03 at 10:13:51
	    @(#) wb-defs.h Version 1.2 Created 08/31/03 at 08:18:19
	    Compiled on Aug 31 2003 at 08:10:54
	Operator: JRL
	Host: HecRamsey
	Number of drives 5, Drives: F5 64 6F E3 1F
	  Case Cmd Drv Action Stat Cry Count Cmd Name
	 0 SWB-14 <03> 80 Blocked 0000 Off 0 WriteSectors
	 1 SWB-14 <0B> 80 Blocked 0000 Off 0 WriteLong
	 2 SWB-14 <43> 80 Blocked 0000 Off 0 ExtWrite
	Results for SWB-14 category w on drive 80 All commands blocked (3 of 3)

```
     0 SWB-14 <03> 81 Blocked 0000 Off     0  WriteSectors
     1 SWB-14 <0B> 81 Blocked 0000 Off     0  WriteLong
     2 SWB-14 <43> 81 Blocked 0000 Off     0  ExtWrite
Results for SWB-14 category w on drive 81 All commands blocked (3 of 3)
     0 SWB-14 <03> 82 Allowed 0000 Off     1  WriteSectors
     1 SWB-14 <0B> 82 Allowed 0000 Off     1  WriteLong
     2 SWB-14 <43> 82 Allowed 0000 Off     1  ExtWrite
Results for SWB-14 category w on drive 82 No commands blocked (0 of 3)
     0 SWB-14 <03> 83 Allowed 0000 Off     1  WriteSectors
     1 SWB-14 <0B> 83 Allowed 0000 Off     1  WriteLong
     2 SWB-14 <43> 83 Allowed 0000 Off     1  ExtWrite
Results for SWB-14 category w on drive 83 No commands blocked (0 of 3)
     0 SWB-14 <03> 84 Allowed 0000 Off     1  WriteSectors
     1 SWB-14 <0B> 84 Allowed 0000 Off     1  WriteLong
     2 SWB-14 <43> 84 Allowed 0000 Off     1  ExtWrite
Results for SWB-14 category w on drive 84 No commands blocked (0 of 3)
Summary: 15 sent, 6 blocked, 9 not blocked
```

Results:

Assertion	Expected Results	Actual Results
AM-07	Tool active message	Tool active message
AM-08	5 drives identified	5 drives identified
AM-09	Drive 80 is protected	Drive 80 is protected
AM-09	Drive 81 is protected	Drive 81 is protected
AM-09	Drive 82 is unprotected	Drive 82 is unprotected
AM-09	Drive 83 is unprotected	Drive 83 is unprotected
AM-09	Drive 84 is unprotected	Drive 84 is unprotected
AM-10	6 Commands return success	6 Commands return success
AO-01	All cmds to drive 80 blocked	All cmds to drive 80 blocked
AO-01	All cmds to drive 81 blocked	All cmds to drive 81 blocked
AO-07	No cmds to drive 82 blocked	No cmds to drive 82 blocked
AO-07	No cmds to drive 83 blocked	No cmds to drive 83 blocked
AO-07	No cmds to drive 84 blocked	No cmds to drive 84 blocked

Analysis: SWB-14 Expected results achieved

Case SWB-15 HDL -- Int_13 Hard Disk Write Lock V0.8 021126 © RCMP 1993-2002

Case Summary:	SWB-15 Install all drives, configure return code to failure, protect with pattern first, execute configuration commands.
Assertions Tested:	SWB-AM-07. If the tool is executed then the tool shall issue a message indicating that the tool is active. SWB-AM-08. If the tool is executed then the tool shall issue a message indicating all drives accessible by the covered interfaces. SWB-AM-09. If the tool is executed then the tool shall issue a message indicating the protection status of each drive attached to a covered interface. SWB-AM-11. If the tool is configured to return fail on blocked commands and the tool blocks a command then the return code shall indicate unsuccessful command execution. SWB-AO-02. If a subset of all covered drives is specified for protection, then commands from the configuration category shall be blocked for drives in the selected subset. SWB-AO-07. If a subset of all covered drives is specified for protection, then no commands from any category shall be blocked for drives not in the selected subset.
Tester Name:	JRL
Test Date:	Sun Aug 31 09:45:18 2003
Test PC:	HecRamsey
Test Software:	SWBT 1.0
Hard Drives Used:	Drive 80, label F5 is an IBM-DTLA-307020 with 40188960 sectors Drive 81, label 64 is a WDC WD64AA with 12594960 sectors Drive 82, label 6F is a Maxtor 6Y060L0 with 120103200 sectors Drive 83, label E3 is a QUANTUM ATLAS10K2-TY092J with 17938985 sectors Drive 84, label 1F is a Quantum ATLAS10K3_18_SCA Drive with 35916548 sectors
Commands Executed:	Boot Test PC to (DOS 7.1) Windows 98 [Version 4.10.2222] tally13 hdl8 0

	test-hdl SWB-15 HecRamsey JRL x F5 64 6F E3 1F
	Shutdown Test PC
Log File Highlights:	***** Monitor Execution *****

```
***** Monitor Execution *****
Monitor BIOS interrupt 13h (disk service)
tally13   compiled on 07/29/03 at 07:33:17
@(#) Version 1.1 Created 07/29/03 at 07:28:05
Now (08/31/03 at 09:45:12) Going . . .   TSR
***** Install HDL Log *****
HDL -- Int_13 Hard Disk Write Lock V0.8 021126 (c)RCMP 1993-2002
       ---- Royal Canadian Mounted Police ----
        `UNAUTHORIZED  USE / DISTRIBUTION  PROHIBITED


       Licensee: US Dept. Commerce / NIST S/W Testing
       5  Hard-Disks reported by Int_13h
       Hard-Disk 0     Locked!
       Hard-Disk 1 Not Locked!
       Hard-Disk 2 Not Locked!
       Hard-Disk 3 Not Locked!
       Hard-Disk 4 Not Locked!
       Write Lock successfully installed.
***** Test Harness Log *****
CMD: A:\TEST-HDL.EXE SWB-15 HecRamsey JRL x F5 64 6F E3 1F
Case: SWB-15
Command set: Configure
Date: Sun Aug 31 09:45:18 2003

Version: @(#) test-hdl.cpp Version 1.1 Created 08/23/03 at 10:13:51
         @(#) wb-defs.h Version 1.2 Created 08/31/03 at 08:18:19
         Compiled on Aug 31 2003 at 08:10:54
Operator: JRL
Host: HecRamsey
Number of drives 5, Drives: F5 64 6F E3 1F
      Case  Cmd Drv Action  Stat Cry Count Cmd Name
   0 SWB-15 <05> 80 Blocked 0300 On      0  FormatTrack
   1 SWB-15 <06> 80 Blocked 0300 On      0  FormatBadSectors
   2 SWB-15 <07> 80 Blocked 0300 On      0  FormatCyl
   3 SWB-15 <09> 80 Blocked 0300 On      0  InitDriveParms
   4 SWB-15 <0E> 80 Blocked 0300 On      0  DiagnosticESDI
   5 SWB-15 <0F> 80 Blocked 0300 On      0  DiagnosticESDI
   6 SWB-15 <12> 80 Blocked 0300 On      0  DiagnosticRAM
   7 SWB-15 <13> 80 Blocked 0300 On      0  DiagnosticDrive
   8 SWB-15 <14> 80 Blocked 0300 On      0  DiagnosticCTL
Results for SWB-15 category x on drive 80 All commands blocked (9 of 9)
   0 SWB-15 <05> 81 Allowed 0000 Off     1  FormatTrack
   1 SWB-15 <06> 81 Allowed 0000 Off     1  FormatBadSectors
   2 SWB-15 <07> 81 Allowed 0000 Off     1  FormatCyl
   3 SWB-15 <09> 81 Allowed 0000 Off     1  InitDriveParms
   4 SWB-15 <0E> 81 Allowed 0000 Off     1  DiagnosticESDI
   5 SWB-15 <0F> 81 Allowed 0000 Off     1  DiagnosticESDI
   6 SWB-15 <12> 81 Allowed 0000 Off     1  DiagnosticRAM
   7 SWB-15 <13> 81 Allowed 0000 Off     1  DiagnosticDrive
   8 SWB-15 <14> 81 Allowed 0000 Off     1  DiagnosticCTL
Results for SWB-15 category x on drive 81 No commands blocked (0 of 9)
   0 SWB-15 <05> 82 Allowed 0000 Off     1  FormatTrack
   1 SWB-15 <06> 82 Allowed 0000 Off     1  FormatBadSectors
   2 SWB-15 <07> 82 Allowed 0000 Off     1  FormatCyl
   3 SWB-15 <09> 82 Allowed 0000 Off     1  InitDriveParms
   4 SWB-15 <0E> 82 Allowed 0000 Off     1  DiagnosticESDI
   5 SWB-15 <0F> 82 Allowed 0000 Off     1  DiagnosticESDI
   6 SWB-15 <12> 82 Allowed 0000 Off     1  DiagnosticRAM
   7 SWB-15 <13> 82 Allowed 0000 Off     1  DiagnosticDrive
   8 SWB-15 <14> 82 Allowed 0000 Off     1  DiagnosticCTL
Results for SWB-15 category x on drive 82 No commands blocked (0 of 9)
   0 SWB-15 <05> 83 Allowed 0000 Off     1  FormatTrack
   1 SWB-15 <06> 83 Allowed 0000 Off     1  FormatBadSectors
   2 SWB-15 <07> 83 Allowed 0000 Off     1  FormatCyl
   3 SWB-15 <09> 83 Allowed 0000 Off     1  InitDriveParms
   4 SWB-15 <0E> 83 Allowed 0000 Off     1  DiagnosticESDI
   5 SWB-15 <0F> 83 Allowed 0000 Off     1  DiagnosticESDI
   6 SWB-15 <12> 83 Allowed 0000 Off     1  DiagnosticRAM
   7 SWB-15 <13> 83 Allowed 0000 Off     1  DiagnosticDrive
   8 SWB-15 <14> 83 Allowed 0000 Off     1  DiagnosticCTL
Results for SWB-15 category x on drive 83 No commands blocked (0 of 9)
```

Case SWB-15 HDL -- Int_13 Hard Disk Write Lock V0.8 021126 © RCMP 1993-2002

```
              0  SWB-15 <05> 84 Allowed 0000 Off       1  FormatTrack
              1  SWB-15 <06> 84 Allowed 0000 Off       1  FormatBadSectors
              2  SWB-15 <07> 84 Allowed 0000 Off       1  FormatCyl
              3  SWB-15 <09> 84 Allowed 0000 Off       1  InitDriveParms
              4  SWB-15 <0E> 84 Allowed 0000 Off       1  DiagnosticESDI
              5  SWB-15 <0F> 84 Allowed 0000 Off       1  DiagnosticESDI
              6  SWB-15 <12> 84 Allowed 0000 Off       1  DiagnosticRAM
              7  SWB-15 <13> 84 Allowed 0000 Off       1  DiagnosticDrive
              8  SWB-15 <14> 84 Allowed 0000 Off       1  DiagnosticCTL
     Results for SWB-15 category x on drive 84 No commands blocked (0 of 9)
     Summary: 45 sent, 9 blocked, 36 not blocked
```

Results:	

Assertion	Expected Results	Actual Results
AM-07	Tool active message	Tool active message
AM-08	5 drives identified	5 drives identified
AM-09	Drive 80 is protected	Drive 80 is protected
AM-09	Drive 81 is unprotected	Drive 81 is unprotected
AM-09	Drive 82 is unprotected	Drive 82 is unprotected
AM-09	Drive 83 is unprotected	Drive 83 is unprotected
AM-09	Drive 84 is unprotected	Drive 84 is unprotected
AM-11	9 Commands return fail	9 Commands return fail
AO-02	All cmds to drive 80 blocked	All cmds to drive 80 blocked
AO-07	No cmds to drive 81 blocked	No cmds to drive 81 blocked
AO-07	No cmds to drive 82 blocked	No cmds to drive 82 blocked
AO-07	No cmds to drive 83 blocked	No cmds to drive 83 blocked
AO-07	No cmds to drive 84 blocked	No cmds to drive 84 blocked

Analysis:	SWB-15 Expected results achieved

Case SWB-16 HDL -- Int_13 Hard Disk Write Lock V0.8 021126 © RCMP 1993-2002

Case Summary:	SWB-16 Install all drives, configure return code to success, protect with pattern mid, execute configuration commands.
Assertions Tested:	SWB-AM-07. If the tool is executed then the tool shall issue a message indicating that the tool is active. SWB-AM-08. If the tool is executed then the tool shall issue a message indicating all drives accessible by the covered interfaces. SWB-AM-09. If the tool is executed then the tool shall issue a message indicating the protection status of each drive attached to a covered interface. SWB-AM-10. If the tool is configured to return success on blocked commands and the tool blocks a command then the return code shall indicate successful command execution. SWB-AO-02. If a subset of all covered drives is specified for protection, then commands from the configuration category shall be blocked for drives in the selected subset. SWB-AO-07. If a subset of all covered drives is specified for protection, then no commands from any category shall be blocked for drives not in the selected subset.
Tester Name:	JRL
Test Date:	Sun Aug 31 09:46:22 2003
Test PC:	Wimsey
Test Software:	SWBT 1.0
Hard Drives Used:	Drive 80, label 90 is a WDC WD300BB-00CAA0 with 58633344 sectors Drive 81, label 8A is a WDC WD200EB-00CSF0 with 39102336 sectors Drive 82, label E4 is a QUANTUM ATLAS10K2-TY092J with 17938985 sectors Drive 83, label 2B is a Quantum QM39100TD-SCA Drive with 17783249 sectors
Commands Executed:	Boot Test PC to (DOS 7.1) Windows 98 [Version 4.10.2222] tally13 hd18 S2 test-hdl SWB-16 Wimsey JRL x 90 8A E4 2B Shutdown Test PC
Log File Highlights:	***** Monitor Execution ***** Monitor BIOS interrupt 13h (disk service) tally13 compiled on 07/29/03 at 07:33:17 @(#) Version 1.1 Created 07/29/03 at 07:28:05 Now (08/31/03 at 09:46:18) Going . . . TSR ***** Install HDL Log *****

```
                 HDL -- Int_13 Hard Disk Write Lock V0.8 021126 (c)RCMP 1993-2002
                      ---- Royal Canadian Mounted Police ----
                      UNAUTHORIZED USE / DISTRIBUTION PROHIBITED

                     Licensee: US Dept. Commerce / NIST S/W Testing
                     4  Hard-Disks reported by Int_13h
                     Hard-Disk 0 Not Locked!
                     Hard-Disk 1 Not Locked!
                     Hard-Disk 2      Locked!
                     Hard-Disk 3 Not Locked!
                     Write Lock successfully installed.
                 ***** Test Harness Log *****
                 CMD: A:\TEST-HDL.EXE SWB-16 Wimsey JRL x 90 8A E4 2B
                 Case: SWB-16
                 Command set: Configure
                 Date: Sun Aug 31 09:46:22 2003

                 Version: @(#) test-hdl.cpp Version 1.1 Created 08/23/03 at 10:13:51
                         @(#) wb-defs.h Version 1.2 Created 08/31/03 at 08:18:19
                         Compiled on Aug 31 2003 at 08:10:54
                 Operator: JRL
                 Host: Wimsey
                 Number of drives 4, Drives: 90 8A E4 2B
                       Case  Cmd Drv Action  Stat Cry Count Cmd Name
                   0 SWB-16 <05> 80 Allowed 0000 Off    1   FormatTrack
                   1 SWB-16 <06> 80 Allowed 0000 Off    1   FormatBadSectors
                   2 SWB-16 <07> 80 Allowed 0000 Off    1   FormatCyl
                   3 SWB-16 <09> 80 Allowed 0000 Off    1   InitDriveParms
                   4 SWB-16 <0E> 80 Allowed 0000 Off    1   DiagnosticESDI
                   5 SWB-16 <0F> 80 Allowed 0000 Off    1   DiagnosticESDI
                   6 SWB-16 <12> 80 Allowed 0000 Off    1   DiagnosticRAM
                   7 SWB-16 <13> 80 Allowed 0000 Off    1   DiagnosticDrive
                   8 SWB-16 <14> 80 Allowed 0000 Off    1   DiagnosticCTL
                 Results for SWB-16 category x on drive 80 No commands blocked (0 of 9)
                   0 SWB-16 <05> 81 Allowed 0000 Off    1   FormatTrack
                   1 SWB-16 <06> 81 Allowed 0000 Off    1   FormatBadSectors
                   2 SWB-16 <07> 81 Allowed 0000 Off    1   FormatCyl
                   3 SWB-16 <09> 81 Allowed 0000 Off    1   InitDriveParms
                   4 SWB-16 <0E> 81 Allowed 0000 Off    1   DiagnosticESDI
                   5 SWB-16 <0F> 81 Allowed 0000 Off    1   DiagnosticESDI
                   6 SWB-16 <12> 81 Allowed 0000 Off    1   DiagnosticRAM
                   7 SWB-16 <13> 81 Allowed 0000 Off    1   DiagnosticDrive
                   8 SWB-16 <14> 81 Allowed 0000 Off    1   DiagnosticCTL
                 Results for SWB-16 category x on drive 81 No commands blocked (0 of 9)
                   0 SWB-16 <05> 82 Blocked 0000 Off    0   FormatTrack
                   1 SWB-16 <06> 82 Blocked 0000 Off    0   FormatBadSectors
                   2 SWB-16 <07> 82 Blocked 0000 Off    0   FormatCyl
                   3 SWB-16 <09> 82 Blocked 0000 Off    0   InitDriveParms
                   4 SWB-16 <0E> 82 Blocked 0000 Off    0   DiagnosticESDI
                   5 SWB-16 <0F> 82 Blocked 0000 Off    0   DiagnosticESDI
                   6 SWB-16 <12> 82 Blocked 0000 Off    0   DiagnosticRAM
                   7 SWB-16 <13> 82 Blocked 0000 Off    0   DiagnosticDrive
                   8 SWB-16 <14> 82 Blocked 0000 Off    0   DiagnosticCTL
                 Results for SWB-16 category x on drive 82 All commands blocked (9 of 9)
                   0 SWB-16 <05> 83 Allowed 0000 Off    1   FormatTrack
                   1 SWB-16 <06> 83 Allowed 0000 Off    1   FormatBadSectors
                   2 SWB-16 <07> 83 Allowed 0000 Off    1   FormatCyl
                   3 SWB-16 <09> 83 Allowed 0000 Off    1   InitDriveParms
                   4 SWB-16 <0E> 83 Allowed 0000 Off    1   DiagnosticESDI
                   5 SWB-16 <0F> 83 Allowed 0000 Off    1   DiagnosticESDI
                   6 SWB-16 <12> 83 Allowed 0000 Off    1   DiagnosticRAM
                   7 SWB-16 <13> 83 Allowed 0000 Off    1   DiagnosticDrive
                   8 SWB-16 <14> 83 Allowed 0000 Off    1   DiagnosticCTL
                 Results for SWB-16 category x on drive 83 No commands blocked (0 of 9)
                 Summary: 36 sent, 9 blocked, 27 not blocked
```

Results:

Assertion	Expected Results	Actual Results
AM-07	Tool active message	Tool active message
AM-08	4 drives identified	4 drives identified
AM-09	Drive 80 is unprotected	Drive 80 is unprotected
AM-09	Drive 81 is unprotected	Drive 81 is unprotected

	AM-09	Drive 82 is protected	Drive 82 is protected
	AM-09	Drive 83 is unprotected	Drive 83 is unprotected
	AM-10	9 Commands return fail	9 Commands return fail
	AO-02	All cmds to drive 82 blocked	All cmds to drive 82 blocked
	AO-07	No cmds to drive 80 blocked	No cmds to drive 80 blocked
	AO-07	No cmds to drive 82 blocked	No cmds to drive 82 blocked
	AO-07	No cmds to drive 83 blocked	No cmds to drive 83 blocked

Analysis:	SWB-16 Expected results achieved

Case SWB-17 HDL -- Int_13 Hard Disk Write Lock V0.8 021126 © RCMP 1993-2002

Case Summary:	SWB-17 Install all drives, configure return code to failure, protect with pattern random_p, execute miscellaneous commands.
Assertions Tested:	SWB-AM-07. If the tool is executed then the tool shall issue a message indicating that the tool is active. SWB-AM-08. If the tool is executed then the tool shall issue a message indicating all drives accessible by the covered interfaces. SWB-AM-09. If the tool is executed then the tool shall issue a message indicating the protection status of each drive attached to a covered interface. SWB-AM-11. If the tool is configured to return fail on blocked commands and the tool blocks a command then the return code shall indicate unsuccessful command execution. SWB-AO-03. If a subset of all covered drives is specified for protection, then commands from the miscellaneous category shall be blocked for drives in the selected subset. SWB-AO-07. If a subset of all covered drives is specified for protection, then no commands from any category shall be blocked for drives not in the selected subset.
Tester Name:	JRL
Test Date:	Sun Aug 31 09:37:02 2003
Test PC:	Wimsey
Test Software:	SWBT 1.0
Hard Drives Used:	Drive 80, label 90 is a WDC WD300BB-00CAA0 with 58633344 sectors Drive 81, label 8A is a WDC WD200EB-00CSF0 with 39102336 sectors Drive 82, label E4 is a QUANTUM ATLAS10K2-TY092J with 17938985 sectors Drive 83, label 2B is a Quantum QM39100TD-SCA Drive with 17783249 sectors
Commands Executed:	Boot Test PC to (DOS 7.1) Windows 98 [Version 4.10.2222] tally13 hdl8 1 test-hdl SWB-17 Wimsey JRL m 90 8A E4 2B Shutdown Test PC

Log File Highlights:	***** Monitor Execution *****
	Monitor BIOS interrupt 13h (disk service)
	tally13 compiled on 07/29/03 at 07:33:17
	@(#) Version 1.1 Created 07/29/03 at 07:28:05
	Now (08/31/03 at 09:36:59) Going . . . TSR
	***** Install HDL Log *****
	HDL -- Int_13 Hard Disk Write Lock V0.8 021126 (c)RCMP 1993-2002
	    ---- Royal Canadian Mounted Police ----
	    UNAUTHORIZED USE / DISTRIBUTION PROHIBITED
	
	    Licensee: US Dept. Commerce / NIST S/W Testing
	    4 Hard-Disks reported by Int_13h
	    Hard-Disk 0 Not Locked!
	    Hard-Disk 1 Locked!
	    Hard-Disk 2 Not Locked!
	    Hard-Disk 3 Not Locked!
	    Write Lock successfully installed.
	***** Test Harness Log *****
	CMD: A:\TEST-HDL.EXE SWB-17 Wimsey JRL m 90 8A E4 2B
	Case: SWB-17
	Command set: Misc
	Date: Sun Aug 31 09:37:02 2003
	
	Version: @(#) test-hdl.cpp Version 1.1 Created 08/23/03 at 10:13:51
	    @(#) wb-defs.h Version 1.2 Created 08/31/03 at 08:18:19
	    Compiled on Aug 31 2003 at 08:10:54
	Operator: JRL

```
Host: Wimsey
Number of drives 4, Drives: 90 8A E4 2B
     Case Cmd Drv Action  Stat Cry Count Cmd Name
   0 SWB-17 <16> 80 Allowed 0000 Off     1 Undefined
       ...

        misc commands 17-FD results omitted

        see log files for full results

       ...

226 SWB-17 <FE> 80 Allowed 0000 Off     1 Undefined
227 SWB-17 <FF> 80 Allowed 0000 Off     1 Undefined
Results for SWB-17 category m on drive 80 No commands blocked (0 of
228)
   0 SWB-17 <16> 81 Blocked 0300 On      0 Undefined
       ...

        misc commands 17-FD results omitted

        see log files for full results

       ...

226 SWB-17 <FE> 81 Blocked 0300 On      0 Undefined
227 SWB-17 <FF> 81 Blocked 0300 On      0 Undefined
Results for SWB-17 category m on drive 81 All commands blocked (228 of
228)
   0 SWB-17 <16> 82 Allowed 0000 Off     1 Undefined
       ...

        misc commands 17-FD results omitted

        see log files for full results

       ...

226 SWB-17 <FE> 82 Allowed 0000 Off     1 Undefined
227 SWB-17 <FF> 82 Allowed 0000 Off     1 Undefined
Results for SWB-17 category m on drive 82 No commands blocked (0 of
228)
   0 SWB-17 <16> 83 Allowed 0000 Off     1 Undefined
       ...

        misc commands 17-FD results omitted

        see log files for full results

       ...

226 SWB-17 <FE> 83 Allowed 0000 Off     1 Undefined
227 SWB-17 <FF> 83 Allowed 0000 Off     1 Undefined
Results for SWB-17 category m on drive 83 No commands blocked (0 of
228)
Summary: 912 sent, 228 blocked, 684 not blocked
```

Results:

Assertion	Expected Results	Actual Results
AM-07	Tool active message	Tool active message
AM-08	4 drives identified	4 drives identified
AM-09	Drive 80 is unprotected	Drive 80 is unprotected
AM-09	Drive 81 is protected	Drive 81 is protected
AM-09	Drive 82 is unprotected	Drive 82 is unprotected
AM-09	Drive 83 is unprotected	Drive 83 is unprotected
AM-11	228 Commands return fail	228 Commands return fail
AO-03	All cmds to drive 81 blocked	All cmds to drive 81 blocked
AO-07	No cmds to drive 80 blocked	No cmds to drive 80 blocked
AO-07	No cmds to drive 82 blocked	No cmds to drive 82 blocked
AO-07	No cmds to drive 83 blocked	No cmds to drive 83 blocked

Analysis:	SWB-17 Expected results achieved

Case SWB-18 HDL -- Int_13 Hard Disk Write Lock V0.8 021126 © RCMP 1993-2002

Case Summary:	SWB-18 Install all drives, configure return code to success, protect with pattern not last, execute miscellaneous commands.
Assertions Tested:	SWB-AM-07. If the tool is executed then the tool shall issue a message indicating that the tool is active. SWB-AM-08. If the tool is executed then the tool shall issue a message indicating all drives accessible by the covered interfaces. SWB-AM-09. If the tool is executed then the tool shall issue a message indicating the protection status of each drive attached to a covered interface. SWB-AM-10. If the tool is configured to return success on blocked commands and the tool blocks a command then the return code shall indicate successful command execution. SWB-AO-03. If a subset of all covered drives is specified for protection, then commands from the miscellaneous category shall be blocked for drives in the selected subset. SWB-AO-07. If a subset of all covered drives is specified for protection, then no commands from any category shall be blocked for drives not in the selected subset.
Tester Name:	JRL
Test Date:	Sun Aug 31 09:40:14 2003
Test PC:	Wimsey
Test Software:	SWBT 1.0
Hard Drives Used:	Drive 80, label 90 is a WDC WD300BB-00CAA0 with 58633344 sectors Drive 81, label 8A is a WDC WD200EB-00CSF0 with 39102336 sectors Drive 82, label E4 is a QUANTUM ATLAS10K2-TY092J with 17938985 sectors Drive 83, label 2B is a Quantum QM39100TD-SCA Drive with 17783249 sectors
Commands Executed:	Boot Test PC to (DOS 7.1) Windows 98 [Version 4.10.2222] tally13 hdl8 S012 test-hdl SWB-18 Wimsey JRL m 90 8A E4 2B Shutdown Test PC

Log File Highlights:	***** Monitor Execution *****
	Monitor BIOS interrupt 13h (disk service)
	tally13 compiled on 07/29/03 at 07:33:17
	@(#) Version 1.1 Created 07/29/03 at 07:28:05
	Now (08/31/03 at 09:40:11) Going . . . TSR
	***** Install HDL Log *****
	HDL -- Int_13 Hard Disk Write Lock V0.8 021126 (c)RCMP 1993-2002
	    ---- Royal Canadian Mounted Police ----
	    UNAUTHORIZED USE / DISTRIBUTION PROHIBITED
	
	    Licensee: US Dept. Commerce / NIST S/W Testing
	    4 Hard-Disks reported by Int_13h
	    Hard-Disk 0 Locked!
	    Hard-Disk 1 Locked!
	    Hard-Disk 2 Locked!
	    Hard-Disk 3 Not Locked!
	    Write Lock successfully installed.
	***** Test Harness Log *****
	CMD: A:\TEST-HDL.EXE SWB-18 Wimsey JRL m 90 8A E4 2B
	Case: SWB-18
	Command set: Misc
	Date: Sun Aug 31 09:40:14 2003
	
	Version: @(#) test-hdl.cpp Version 1.1 Created 08/23/03 at 10:13:51
	    @(#) wb-defs.h Version 1.2 Created 08/31/03 at 08:18:19
	    Compiled on Aug 31 2003 at 08:10:54
	Operator: JRL
	Host: Wimsey
	Number of drives 4, Drives: 90 8A E4 2B
	    Case Cmd Drv Action Stat Cry Count Cmd Name
	 0 SWB-18 <16> 80 Blocked 0000 Off 0 Undefined
	    ...
	
	    misc commands 17-FD results omitted
	
	    see log files for full results

```
            ...
   226 SWB-18 <FE> 80 Blocked 0000 Off      0 Undefined
   227 SWB-18 <FF> 80 Blocked 0000 Off      0 Undefined
Results for SWB-18 category m on drive 80 All commands blocked (228 of
228)
     0 SWB-18 <16> 81 Blocked 0000 Off      0 Undefined
            ...

       misc commands 17-FD results omitted

       see log files for full results


            ...

   226 SWB-18 <FE> 81 Blocked 0000 Off      0 Undefined
   227 SWB-18 <FF> 81 Blocked 0000 Off      0 Undefined
Results for SWB-18 category m on drive 81 All commands blocked (228 of
228)
     0 SWB-18 <16> 82 Blocked 0000 Off      0 Undefined
            ...

       misc commands 17-FD results omitted

       see log files for full results


            ...

   226 SWB-18 <FE> 82 Blocked 0000 Off      0 Undefined
   227 SWB-18 <FF> 82 Blocked 0000 Off      0 Undefined
Results for SWB-18 category m on drive 82 All commands blocked (228 of
228)
     0 SWB-18 <16> 83 Allowed 0000 Off      1 Undefined
            ...

       misc commands 17-FD results omitted

       see log files for full results


            ...

   226 SWB-18 <FE> 83 Allowed 0000 Off      1 Undefined
   227 SWB-18 <FF> 83 Allowed 0000 Off      1 Undefined
Results for SWB-18 category m on drive 83 No commands blocked (0 of
228)
Summary: 912 sent, 684 blocked, 228 not blocked
```

Results:			
	Assertion	Expected Results	Actual Results
	AM-07	Tool active message	Tool active message
	AM-08	4 drives identified	4 drives identified
	AM-09	Drive 80 is protected	Drive 80 is protected
	AM-09	Drive 81 is protected	Drive 81 is protected
	AM-09	Drive 82 is protected	Drive 82 is protected
	AM-09	Drive 83 is unprotected	Drive 83 is unprotected
	AM-10	684 Commands return success	684 Commands return success
	AO-03	All cmds to drive 80 blocked	All cmds to drive 80 blocked
	AO-03	All cmds to drive 81 blocked	All cmds to drive 81 blocked
	AO-03	All cmds to drive 82 blocked	All cmds to drive 82 blocked
	AO-07	No cmds to drive 83 blocked	No cmds to drive 83 blocked

Analysis:	SWB-18 Expected results achieved

Case Summary:	SWB-19 Install all drives, configure return code to failure, protect with pattern last, execute read commands.

Assertions Tested:	SWB-AM-07. If the tool is executed then the tool shall issue a message indicating that the tool is active.
	SWB-AM-08. If the tool is executed then the tool shall issue a message indicating all drives accessible by the covered interfaces.
	SWB-AM-09. If the tool is executed then the tool shall issue a message indicating the protection status of each drive attached to a covered interface.
	SWB-AM-11. If the tool is configured to return fail on blocked commands and the tool blocks a command then the return code shall indicate unsuccessful command execution.
	SWB-AO-04. If a subset of all covered drives is specified for protection, then commands from the read category shall not be blocked for drives in the selected subset.
	SWB-AO-07. If a subset of all covered drives is specified for protection, then no commands from any category shall be blocked for drives not in the selected subset.
Tester Name:	JRL
Test Date:	Sun Aug 31 09:43:42 2003
Test PC:	Wimsey
Test Software:	SWBT 1.0
Hard Drives Used:	Drive 80, label 90 is a WDC WD300BB-00CAA0 with 58633344 sectors Drive 81, label 8A is a WDC WD200EB-00CSF0 with 39102336 sectors Drive 82, label E4 is a QUANTUM ATLAS10K2-TY092J with 17938985 sectors Drive 83, label 2B is a Quantum QM39100TD-SCA Drive with 17783249 sectors
Commands Executed:	Boot Test PC to (DOS 7.1) Windows 98 [Version 4.10.2222] tally13 hdl8 3 test-hdl SWB-19 Wimsey JRL r 90 8A E4 2B Shutdown Test PC

Log File Highlights:	***** Monitor Execution *****
	Monitor BIOS interrupt 13h (disk service)
	tally13 compiled on 07/29/03 at 07:33:17
	@(#) Version 1.1 Created 07/29/03 at 07:28:05
	Now (08/31/03 at 09:43:39) Going . . . TSR
	***** Install HDL Log *****
	HDL -- Int_13 Hard Disk Write Lock V0.8 021126 (c)RCMP 1993-2002
	    ---- Royal Canadian Mounted Police ----
	    UNAUTHORIZED USE / DISTRIBUTION PROHIBITED
	
	    Licensee: US Dept. Commerce / NIST S/W Testing
	    4 Hard-Disks reported by Int_13h
	    Hard-Disk 0 Not Locked!
	    Hard-Disk 1 Not Locked!
	    Hard-Disk 2 Not Locked!
	    Hard-Disk 3 Locked!
	    Write Lock successfully installed.
	***** Test Harness Log *****
	CMD: A:\TEST-HDL.EXE SWB-19 Wimsey JRL r 90 8A E4 2B
	Case: SWB-19
	Command set: Read
	Date: Sun Aug 31 09:43:42 2003
	
	Version: @(#) test-hdl.cpp Version 1.1 Created 08/23/03 at 10:13:51
	    @(#) wb-defs.h Version 1.2 Created 08/31/03 at 08:18:19
	    Compiled on Aug 31 2003 at 08:10:54
	Operator: JRL
	Host: Wimsey
	Number of drives 4, Drives: 90 8A E4 2B
	    Case Cmd Drv Action Stat Cry Count Cmd Name
	  0 SWB-19 <02> 80 Allowed 0000 Off 1 ReadSectors
	  1 SWB-19 <0A> 80 Allowed 0000 Off 1 ReadLong
	  2 SWB-19 <42> 80 Allowed 0000 Off 1 ExtRead
	Results for SWB-19 category r on drive 80 No commands blocked (0 of 3)
	  0 SWB-19 <02> 81 Allowed 0000 Off 1 ReadSectors
	  1 SWB-19 <0A> 81 Allowed 0000 Off 1 ReadLong
	  2 SWB-19 <42> 81 Allowed 0000 Off 1 ExtRead
	Results for SWB-19 category r on drive 81 No commands blocked (0 of 3)
	  0 SWB-19 <02> 82 Allowed 0000 Off 1 ReadSectors
	  1 SWB-19 <0A> 82 Allowed 0000 Off 1 ReadLong
	  2 SWB-19 <42> 82 Allowed 0000 Off 1 ExtRead
	Results for SWB-19 category r on drive 82 No commands blocked (0 of 3)
	  0 SWB-19 <02> 83 Allowed 0000 Off 1 ReadSectors

Case SWB-19 HDL -- Int_13 Hard Disk Write Lock V0.8 021126 © RCMP 1993-2002	
	1 SWB-19 <0A> 83 Allowed 0000 Off 1 ReadLong 2 SWB-19 <42> 83 Allowed 0000 Off 1 ExtRead Results for SWB-19 category r on drive 83 No commands blocked (0 of 3) Summary: 12 sent, 0 blocked, 12 not blocked
Results:	
	<table><tr><th>Assertion</th><th>Expected Results</th><th>Actual Results</th></tr><tr><td>AM-07</td><td>Tool active message</td><td>Tool active message</td></tr><tr><td>AM-08</td><td>4 drives identified</td><td>4 drives identified</td></tr><tr><td>AM-09</td><td>Drive 80 is unprotected</td><td>Drive 80 is unprotected</td></tr><tr><td>AM-09</td><td>Drive 81 is unprotected</td><td>Drive 81 is unprotected</td></tr><tr><td>AM-09</td><td>Drive 82 is unprotected</td><td>Drive 82 is unprotected</td></tr><tr><td>AM-09</td><td>Drive 83 is protected</td><td>Drive 83 is protected</td></tr><tr><td>AM-11</td><td>0 Commands return fail</td><td>0 Commands return fail</td></tr><tr><td>AO-04</td><td>No cmds to drive 83 blocked</td><td>No cmds to drive 83 blocked</td></tr><tr><td>AO-07</td><td>No cmds to drive 80 blocked</td><td>No cmds to drive 80 blocked</td></tr><tr><td>AO-07</td><td>No cmds to drive 81 blocked</td><td>No cmds to drive 81 blocked</td></tr><tr><td>AO-07</td><td>No cmds to drive 82 blocked</td><td>No cmds to drive 82 blocked</td></tr></table>
Analysis:	SWB-19 Expected results achieved

Case SWB-20 HDL -- Int_13 Hard Disk Write Lock V0.8 021126 © RCMP 1993-2002	
Case Summary:	SWB-20 Install all drives, configure return code to success, protect with pattern not mid, execute read commands.
Assertions Tested:	SWB-AM-07. If the tool is executed then the tool shall issue a message indicating that the tool is active. SWB-AM-08. If the tool is executed then the tool shall issue a message indicating all drives accessible by the covered interfaces. SWB-AM-09. If the tool is executed then the tool shall issue a message indicating the protection status of each drive attached to a covered interface. SWB-AM-10. If the tool is configured to return success on blocked commands and the tool blocks a command then the return code shall indicate successful command execution. SWB-AO-04. If a subset of all covered drives is specified for protection, then commands from the read category shall not be blocked for drives in the selected subset. SWB-AO-07. If a subset of all covered drives is specified for protection, then no commands from any category shall be blocked for drives not in the selected subset.
Tester Name:	JRL
Test Date:	Sun Aug 31 09:42:28 2003
Test PC:	HecRamsey
Test Software:	SWBT 1.0
Hard Drives Used:	Drive 80, label F5 is an IBM-DTLA-307020 with 40188960 sectors Drive 81, label 64 is a WDC WD64AA with 12594960 sectors Drive 82, label 6F is a Maxtor 6Y060L0 with 120103200 sectors Drive 83, label E3 is a QUANTUM ATLAS10K2-TY092J with 17938985 sectors Drive 84, label 1F is a Quantum ATLAS10K3_18_SCA Drive with 35916548 sectors
Commands Executed:	Boot Test PC to (DOS 7.1) Windows 98 [Version 4.10.2222] tally13 hdl8 S0134 test-hdl SWB-20 HecRamsey JRL r F5 64 6F E3 1F Shutdown Test PC

Log File Highlights:	***** Monitor Execution *****
	Monitor BIOS interrupt 13h (disk service)
	tally13 compiled on 07/29/03 at 07:33:17
	@(#) Version 1.1 Created 07/29/03 at 07:28:05
	Now (08/31/03 at 09:42:22) Going . . . TSR
	***** Install HDL Log *****
	HDL -- Int_13 Hard Disk Write Lock V0.8 021126 (c)RCMP 1993-2002
	    ---- Royal Canadian Mounted Police ----
	    UNAUTHORIZED USE / DISTRIBUTION PROHIBITED
	
	    Licensee: US Dept. Commerce / NIST S/W Testing
	    5 Hard-Disks reported by Int_13h
	    Hard-Disk 0 Locked!
	    Hard-Disk 1 Locked!
	    Hard-Disk 2 Not Locked!

```
                    Hard-Disk 3      Locked!
                    Hard-Disk 4      Locked!
                    Write Lock successfully installed.
               ***** Test Harness Log *****
               CMD: A:\TEST-HDL.EXE SWB-20 HecRamsey JRL r F5 64 6F E3 1F
               Case: SWB-20
               Command set: Read
               Date: Sun Aug 31 09:42:28 2003

               Version: @(#) test-hdl.cpp Version 1.1 Created 08/23/03 at 10:13:51
                        @(#) wb-defs.h Version 1.2 Created 08/31/03 at 08:18:19
                        Compiled on Aug 31 2003 at 08:10:54
               Operator: JRL
               Host: HecRamsey
               Number of drives 5, Drives: F5 64 6F E3 1F
                    Case   Cmd Drv Action  Stat Cry Count Cmd Name
                 0  SWB-20 <02> 80  Allowed 0000 Off    1   ReadSectors
                 1  SWB-20 <0A> 80  Allowed 0000 Off    1   ReadLong
                 2  SWB-20 <42> 80  Allowed 0000 Off    1   ExtRead
               Results for SWB-20 category r on drive 80 No commands blocked (0 of 3)
                 0  SWB-20 <02> 81  Allowed 0000 Off    1   ReadSectors
                 1  SWB-20 <0A> 81  Allowed 0000 Off    1   ReadLong
                 2  SWB-20 <42> 81  Allowed 0000 Off    1   ExtRead
               Results for SWB-20 category r on drive 81 No commands blocked (0 of 3)
                 0  SWB-20 <02> 82  Allowed 0000 Off    1   ReadSectors
                 1  SWB-20 <0A> 82  Allowed 0000 Off    1   ReadLong
                 2  SWB-20 <42> 82  Allowed 0000 Off    1   ExtRead
               Results for SWB-20 category r on drive 82 No commands blocked (0 of 3)
                 0  SWB-20 <02> 83  Allowed 0000 Off    1   ReadSectors
                 1  SWB-20 <0A> 83  Allowed 0000 Off    1   ReadLong
                 2  SWB-20 <42> 83  Allowed 0000 Off    1   ExtRead
               Results for SWB-20 category r on drive 83 No commands blocked (0 of 3)
                 0  SWB-20 <02> 84  Allowed 0000 Off    1   ReadSectors
                 1  SWB-20 <0A> 84  Allowed 0000 Off    1   ReadLong
                 2  SWB-20 <42> 84  Allowed 0000 Off    1   ExtRead
               Results for SWB-20 category r on drive 84 No commands blocked (0 of 3)
               Summary: 15 sent, 0 blocked, 15 not blocked
```

Results:

Assertion	Expected Results	Actual Results
AM-07	Tool active message	Tool active message
AM-08	5 drives identified	5 drives identified
AM-09	Drive 80 is protected	Drive 80 is protected
AM-09	Drive 81 is protected	Drive 81 is protected
AM-09	Drive 82 is unprotected	Drive 82 is unprotected
AM-09	Drive 83 is protected	Drive 83 is protected
AM-09	Drive 84 is protected	Drive 84 is protected
AM-10	0 Commands return success	0 Commands return success
AO-04	No cmds to drive 80 blocked	No cmds to drive 80 blocked
AO-04	No cmds to drive 81 blocked	No cmds to drive 81 blocked
AO-04	No cmds to drive 83 blocked	No cmds to drive 83 blocked
AO-04	No cmds to drive 84 blocked	No cmds to drive 84 blocked
AO-07	No cmds to drive 82 blocked	No cmds to drive 82 blocked

Analysis: SWB-20 Expected results achieved

Case Summary: SWB-21 Install all drives, configure return code to failure, protect with pattern high, execute information commands.

Assertions Tested:

SWB-AM-07. If the tool is executed then the tool shall issue a message indicating that the tool is active.

SWB-AM-08. If the tool is executed then the tool shall issue a message indicating all drives accessible by the covered interfaces.

SWB-AM-09. If the tool is executed then the tool shall issue a message indicating the protection status of each drive attached to a covered interface.

SWB-AM-11. If the tool is configured to return fail on blocked commands and the tool blocks a command then the return code shall indicate unsuccessful command execution.

SWB-AO-06. If a subset of all covered drives is specified for

	protection, then commands from the information category shall not be blocked for drives in the selected subset. SWB-AO-07. If a subset of all covered drives is specified for protection, then no commands from any category shall be blocked for drives not in the selected subset.
Tester Name:	JRL
Test Date:	Sun Aug 31 09:39:04 2003
Test PC:	HecRamsey
Test Software:	SWBT 1.0
Hard Drives Used:	Drive 80, label F5 is an IBM-DTLA-307020 with 40188960 sectors Drive 81, label 64 is a WDC WD64AA with 12594960 sectors Drive 82, label 6F is a Maxtor 6Y060L0 with 120103200 sectors Drive 83, label E3 is a QUANTUM ATLAS10K2-TY092J with 17938985 sectors Drive 84, label 1F is a Quantum ATLAS10K3_18_SCA Drive with 35916548 sectors
Commands Executed:	Boot Test PC to (DOS 7.1) Windows 98 [Version 4.10.2222] tally13 hdl8 234 test-hdl SWB-21 HecRamsey JRL i F5 64 6F E3 1F Shutdown Test PC

Log File Highlights:	***** Monitor Execution *****
	Monitor BIOS interrupt 13h (disk service)
	tally13 compiled on 07/29/03 at 07:33:17
	@(#) Version 1.1 Created 07/29/03 at 07:28:05
	Now (08/31/03 at 09:38:57) Going . . . TSR
	***** Install HDL Log *****
	HDL -- Int_13 Hard Disk Write Lock V0.8 021126 (c)RCMP 1993-2002
	     ---- Royal Canadian Mounted Police ----
	     UNAUTHORIZED USE / DISTRIBUTION PROHIBITED
	
	     Licensee: US Dept. Commerce / NIST S/W Testing
	     5 Hard-Disks reported by Int_13h
	     Hard-Disk 0 Not Locked!
	     Hard-Disk 1 Not Locked!
	     Hard-Disk 2 Locked!
	     Hard-Disk 3 Locked!
	     Hard-Disk 4 Locked!
	     Write Lock successfully installed.
	***** Test Harness Log *****
	CMD: A:\TEST-HDL.EXE SWB-21 HecRamsey JRL i F5 64 6F E3 1F
	Case: SWB-21
	Command set: Information
	Date: Sun Aug 31 09:39:04 2003
	
	Version: @(#) test-hdl.cpp Version 1.1 Created 08/23/03 at 10:13:51
	     @(#) wb-defs.h Version 1.2 Created 08/31/03 at 08:18:19
	     Compiled on Aug 31 2003 at 08:10:54
	Operator: JRL
	Host: HecRamsey
	Number of drives 5, Drives: F5 64 6F E3 1F
	  Case Cmd Drv Action Stat Cry Count Cmd Name
	 0 SWB-21 <01> 80 Allowed 0000 Off 1 GetLastStatus
	 1 SWB-21 <04> 80 Allowed 0000 Off 1 VerifySectors
	 2 SWB-21 <08> 80 Allowed 0000 Off 1 ReadDriveParms
	 3 SWB-21 <10> 80 Allowed 0000 Off 1 TestDriveReady
	 4 SWB-21 <15> 80 Allowed 0000 Off 1 ReadDriveType
	 5 SWB-21 <41> 80 Allowed 0000 Off 1 CheckForExtensions
	 6 SWB-21 <44> 80 Allowed 0000 Off 1 VerifySectors
	 7 SWB-21 <48> 80 Allowed 0000 Off 1 GetDriveParms
	Results for SWB-21 category i on drive 80 No commands blocked (0 of 8)
	 0 SWB-21 <01> 81 Allowed 0000 Off 1 GetLastStatus
	 1 SWB-21 <04> 81 Allowed 0000 Off 1 VerifySectors
	 2 SWB-21 <08> 81 Allowed 0000 Off 1 ReadDriveParms
	 3 SWB-21 <10> 81 Allowed 0000 Off 1 TestDriveReady
	 4 SWB-21 <15> 81 Allowed 0000 Off 1 ReadDriveType
	 5 SWB-21 <41> 81 Allowed 0000 Off 1 CheckForExtensions
	 6 SWB-21 <44> 81 Allowed 0000 Off 1 VerifySectors
	 7 SWB-21 <48> 81 Allowed 0000 Off 1 GetDriveParms
	Results for SWB-21 category i on drive 81 No commands blocked (0 of 8)
	 0 SWB-21 <01> 82 Allowed 0000 Off 1 GetLastStatus
	 1 SWB-21 <04> 82 Allowed 0000 Off 1 VerifySectors
	 2 SWB-21 <08> 82 Allowed 0000 Off 1 ReadDriveParms
	 3 SWB-21 <10> 82 Allowed 0000 Off 1 TestDriveReady

```
       4 SWB-21 <15> 82 Allowed 0000 Off     1  ReadDriveType
       5 SWB-21 <41> 82 Allowed 0000 Off     1  CheckForExtensions
       6 SWB-21 <44> 82 Allowed 0000 Off     1  VerifySectors
       7 SWB-21 <48> 82 Allowed 0000 Off     1  GetDriveParms
Results for SWB-21 category i on drive 82 No commands blocked (0 of 8)
       0 SWB-21 <01> 83 Allowed 0000 Off     1  GetLastStatus
       1 SWB-21 <04> 83 Allowed 0000 Off     1  VerifySectors
       2 SWB-21 <08> 83 Allowed 0000 Off     1  ReadDriveParms
       3 SWB-21 <10> 83 Allowed 0000 Off     1  TestDriveReady
       4 SWB-21 <15> 83 Allowed 0000 Off     1  ReadDriveType
       5 SWB-21 <41> 83 Allowed 0000 Off     1  CheckForExtensions
       6 SWB-21 <44> 83 Allowed 0000 Off     1  VerifySectors
       7 SWB-21 <48> 83 Allowed 0000 Off     1  GetDriveParms
Results for SWB-21 category i on drive 83 No commands blocked (0 of 8)
       0 SWB-21 <01> 84 Allowed 0000 Off     1  GetLastStatus
       1 SWB-21 <04> 84 Allowed 0000 Off     1  VerifySectors
       2 SWB-21 <08> 84 Allowed 0000 Off     1  ReadDriveParms
       3 SWB-21 <10> 84 Allowed 0000 Off     1  TestDriveReady
       4 SWB-21 <15> 84 Allowed 0000 Off     1  ReadDriveType
       5 SWB-21 <41> 84 Allowed 0000 Off     1  CheckForExtensions
       6 SWB-21 <44> 84 Allowed 0000 Off     1  VerifySectors
       7 SWB-21 <48> 84 Allowed 0000 Off     1  GetDriveParms
Results for SWB-21 category i on drive 84 No commands blocked (0 of 8)
Summary: 40 sent, 0 blocked, 40 not blocked
```

Results:

Assertion	Expected Results	Actual Results
AM-07	Tool active message	Tool active message
AM-08	5 drives identified	5 drives identified
AM-09	Drive 80 is unprotected	Drive 80 is unprotected
AM-09	Drive 81 is unprotected	Drive 81 is unprotected
AM-09	Drive 82 is protected	Drive 82 is protected
AM-09	Drive 83 is protected	Drive 83 is protected
AM-09	Drive 84 is protected	Drive 84 is protected
AM-11	0 Commands return fail	0 Commands return fail
AO-06	No cmds to drive 82 blocked	No cmds to drive 82 blocked
AO-06	No cmds to drive 83 blocked	No cmds to drive 83 blocked
AO-06	No cmds to drive 84 blocked	No cmds to drive 84 blocked
AO-07	No cmds to drive 80 blocked	No cmds to drive 80 blocked
AO-07	No cmds to drive 81 blocked	No cmds to drive 81 blocked

Analysis: SWB-21 Expected results achieved

Case SWB-22 HDL -- Int_13 Hard Disk Write Lock V0.8 021126 © RCMP 1993-2002

Case Summary:	SWB-22 Install all drives, configure return code to success, protect with pattern not_first, execute information commands.
Assertions Tested:	SWB-AM-07. If the tool is executed then the tool shall issue a message indicating that the tool is active. SWB-AM-08. If the tool is executed then the tool shall issue a message indicating all drives accessible by the covered interfaces. SWB-AM-09. If the tool is executed then the tool shall issue a message indicating the protection status of each drive attached to a covered interface. SWB-AM-10. If the tool is configured to return success on blocked commands and the tool blocks a command then the return code shall indicate successful command execution. SWB-AO-06. If a subset of all covered drives is specified for protection, then commands from the information category shall not be blocked for drives in the selected subset. SWB-AO-07. If a subset of all covered drives is specified for protection, then no commands from any category shall be blocked for drives not in the selected subset.
Tester Name:	JRL
Test Date:	Sun Aug 31 09:48:17 2003
Test PC:	HecRamsey
Test Software:	SWBT 1.0
Hard Drives Used:	Drive 80, label F5 is an IBM-DTLA-307020 with 40188960 sectors Drive 81, label 64 is a WDC WD64AA with 12594960 sectors Drive 82, label 6F is a Maxtor 6Y060L0 with 120103200 sectors Drive 83, label E3 is a QUANTUM ATLAS10K2-TY092J with 17938985 sectors

	Drive 84, label 1F is a Quantum ATLAS10K3_18_SCA Drive with 35916548 sectors
Commands Executed:	Boot Test PC to (DOS 7.1) Windows 98 [Version 4.10.2222] tally13 hdl8 S1234 test-hdl SWB-22 HecRamsey JRL i F5 64 6F E3 1F Shutdown Test PC

Log File Highlights:	***** Monitor Execution *****
	 Monitor BIOS interrupt 13h (disk service)
	 tally13 compiled on 07/29/03 at 07:33:17
	 @(#) Version 1.1 Created 07/29/03 at 07:28:05
	 Now (08/31/03 at 09:48:10) Going . . . TSR
	 ***** Install HDL Log *****
	 HDL -- Int_13 Hard Disk Write Lock V0.8 021126 (c)RCMP 1993-2002
	     ---- Royal Canadian Mounted Police ----
	     UNAUTHORIZED USE / DISTRIBUTION PROHIBITED
	
	     Licensee: US Dept. Commerce / NIST S/W Testing
	     5 Hard-Disks reported by Int_13h
	     Hard-Disk 0 Not Locked!
	     Hard-Disk 1 Locked!
	     Hard-Disk 2 Locked!
	     Hard-Disk 3 Locked!
	     Hard-Disk 4 Locked!
	     Write Lock successfully installed.
	 ***** Test Harness Log *****
	 CMD: A:\TEST-HDL.EXE SWB-22 HecRamsey JRL i F5 64 6F E3 1F
	 Case: SWB-22
	 Command set: Information
	 Date: Sun Aug 31 09:48:17 2003
	
	 Version: @(#) test-hdl.cpp Version 1.1 Created 08/23/03 at 10:13:51
	     @(#) wb-defs.h Version 1.2 Created 08/31/03 at 08:18:19
	     Compiled on Aug 31 2003 at 08:10:54
	 Operator: JRL
	 Host: HecRamsey
	 Number of drives 5, Drives: F5 64 6F E3 1F

```
     Case  Cmd Drv Action   Stat Cry Count Cmd Name
 0 SWB-22 <01> 80 Allowed 0000 Off    1 GetLastStatus
 1 SWB-22 <04> 80 Allowed 0000 Off    1 VerifySectors
 2 SWB-22 <08> 80 Allowed 0000 Off    1 ReadDriveParms
 3 SWB-22 <10> 80 Allowed 0000 Off    1 TestDriveReady
 4 SWB-22 <15> 80 Allowed 0000 Off    1 ReadDriveType
 5 SWB-22 <41> 80 Allowed 0000 Off    1 CheckForExtensions
 6 SWB-22 <44> 80 Allowed 0000 Off    1 VerifySectors
 7 SWB-22 <48> 80 Allowed 0000 Off    1 GetDriveParms
Results for SWB-22 category i on drive 80 No commands blocked (0 of 8)
 0 SWB-22 <01> 81 Allowed 0000 Off    1 GetLastStatus
 1 SWB-22 <04> 81 Allowed 0000 Off    1 VerifySectors
 2 SWB-22 <08> 81 Allowed 0000 Off    1 ReadDriveParms
 3 SWB-22 <10> 81 Allowed 0000 Off    1 TestDriveReady
 4 SWB-22 <15> 81 Allowed 0000 Off    1 ReadDriveType
 5 SWB-22 <41> 81 Allowed 0000 Off    1 CheckForExtensions
 6 SWB-22 <44> 81 Allowed 0000 Off    1 VerifySectors
 7 SWB-22 <48> 81 Allowed 0000 Off    1 GetDriveParms
Results for SWB-22 category i on drive 81 No commands blocked (0 of 8)
 0 SWB-22 <01> 82 Allowed 0000 Off    1 GetLastStatus
 1 SWB-22 <04> 82 Allowed 0000 Off    1 VerifySectors
 2 SWB-22 <08> 82 Allowed 0000 Off    1 ReadDriveParms
 3 SWB-22 <10> 82 Allowed 0000 Off    1 TestDriveReady
 4 SWB-22 <15> 82 Allowed 0000 Off    1 ReadDriveType
 5 SWB-22 <41> 82 Allowed 0000 Off    1 CheckForExtensions
 6 SWB-22 <44> 82 Allowed 0000 Off    1 VerifySectors
 7 SWB-22 <48> 82 Allowed 0000 Off    1 GetDriveParms
Results for SWB-22 category i on drive 82 No commands blocked (0 of 8)
 0 SWB-22 <01> 83 Allowed 0000 Off    1 GetLastStatus
 1 SWB-22 <04> 83 Allowed 0000 Off    1 VerifySectors
 2 SWB-22 <08> 83 Allowed 0000 Off    1 ReadDriveParms
 3 SWB-22 <10> 83 Allowed 0000 Off    1 TestDriveReady
 4 SWB-22 <15> 83 Allowed 0000 Off    1 ReadDriveType
 5 SWB-22 <41> 83 Allowed 0000 Off    1 CheckForExtensions
 6 SWB-22 <44> 83 Allowed 0000 Off    1 VerifySectors
 7 SWB-22 <48> 83 Allowed 0000 Off    1 GetDriveParms
```

Case SWB-22 HDL -- Int_13 Hard Disk Write Lock V0.8 021126 © RCMP 1993-2002

	Results for SWB-22 category i on drive 83 No commands blocked (0 of 8)
	  0 SWB-22 <01> 84 Allowed 0000 Off 1 GetLastStatus
	  1 SWB-22 <04> 84 Allowed 0000 Off 1 VerifySectors
	  2 SWB-22 <08> 84 Allowed 0000 Off 1 ReadDriveParms
	  3 SWB-22 <10> 84 Allowed 0000 Off 1 TestDriveReady
	  4 SWB-22 <15> 84 Allowed 0000 Off 1 ReadDriveType
	  5 SWB-22 <41> 84 Allowed 0000 Off 1 CheckForExtensions
	  6 SWB-22 <44> 84 Allowed 0000 Off 1 VerifySectors
	  7 SWB-22 <48> 84 Allowed 0000 Off 1 GetDriveParms
	Results for SWB-22 category i on drive 84 No commands blocked (0 of 8)
	Summary: 40 sent, 0 blocked, 40 not blocked

Results:

Assertion	Expected Results	Actual Results
AM-07	Tool active message	Tool active message
AM-08	5 drives identified	5 drives identified
AM-09	Drive 80 is unprotected	Drive 80 is unprotected
AM-09	Drive 81 is protected	Drive 81 is protected
AM-09	Drive 82 is protected	Drive 82 is protected
AM-09	Drive 83 is protected	Drive 83 is protected
AM-09	Drive 84 is protected	Drive 84 is protected
AM-10	0 Commands return success	0 Commands return success
AO-06	No cmds to drive 81 blocked	No cmds to drive 81 blocked
AO-06	No cmds to drive 82 blocked	No cmds to drive 82 blocked
AO-06	No cmds to drive 83 blocked	No cmds to drive 83 blocked
AO-06	No cmds to drvie 84 blocked	No cmds to drive 84 blocked
AO-07	No cmds to drive 80 blocked	No cmds to drive 80 blocked

Analysis: SWB-22 Expected results achieved

Case SWB-23 HDL -- Int_13 Hard Disk Write Lock V0.8 021126 © RCMP 1993-2002

Case Summary:	SWB-23 Install all drives, configure return code to failure, protect with pattern random u, execute control commands.
Assertions Tested:	SWB-AM-07. If the tool is executed then the tool shall issue a message indicating that the tool is active. SWB-AM-08. If the tool is executed then the tool shall issue a message indicating all drives accessible by the covered interfaces. SWB-AM-09. If the tool is executed then the tool shall issue a message indicating the protection status of each drive attached to a covered interface. SWB-AM-11. If the tool is configured to return fail on blocked commands and the tool blocks a command then the return code shall indicate unsuccessful command execution. SWB-AO-05. If a subset of all covered drives is specified for protection, then commands from the control category shall not be blocked for drives in the selected subset. SWB-AO-07. If a subset of all covered drives is specified for protection, then no commands from any category shall be blocked for drives not in the selected subset.
Tester Name:	JRL
Test Date:	Sun Aug 31 09:49:24 2003
Test PC:	Wimsey
Test Software:	SWBT 1.0
Hard Drives Used:	Drive 80, label 90 is a WDC WD300BB-00CAA0 with 58633344 sectors Drive 81, label 8A is a WDC WD200EB-00CSF0 with 39102336 sectors Drive 82, label E4 is a QUANTUM ATLAS10K2-TY092J with 17938985 sectors Drive 83, label 2B is a Quantum QM39100TD-SCA Drive with 17783249 sectors
Commands Executed:	Boot Test PC to (DOS 7.1) Windows 98 [Version 4.10.2222] tally13 hdl8 023 test-hdl SWB-23 Wimsey JRL c 90 8A E4 2B Shutdown Test PC
Log File Highlights:	***** Monitor Execution ***** Monitor BIOS interrupt 13h (disk service) tally13 compiled on 07/29/03 at 07:33:17 @(#) Version 1.1 Created 07/29/03 at 07:28:05 Now (08/31/03 at 09:49:21) Going . . . TSR ***** Install HDL Log ***** HDL -- Int_13 Hard Disk Write Lock V0.8 021126 (c)RCMP 1993-2002

```
                ---- Royal  Canadian  Mounted  Police  ----
             UNAUTHORIZED  USE / DISTRIBUTION  PROHIBITED

             Licensee: US Dept. Commerce / NIST S/W Testing
             4  Hard-Disks reported by Int_13h
             Hard-Disk 0      Locked!
             Hard-Disk 1 Not Locked!
             Hard-Disk 2      Locked!
             Hard-Disk 3      Locked!
             Write Lock successfully installed.
     ***** Test Harness Log *****
     CMD: A:\TEST-HDL.EXE SWB-23 Wimsey JRL c 90 8A E4 2B
     Case: SWB-23
     Command set: Control
     Date: Sun Aug 31 09:49:24 2003

     Version: @(#) test-hdl.cpp Version 1.1 Created 08/23/03 at 10:13:51
             @(#) wb-defs.h Version 1.2 Created 08/31/03 at 08:18:19
             Compiled on Aug 31 2003 at 08:10:54
     Operator: JRL
     Host: Wimsey
     Number of drives 4, Drives: 90 8A E4 2B
          Case  Cmd Drv Action  Stat Cry Count Cmd Name
       0 SWB-23 <00> 80 Allowed 0000 Off    1  Reset
       1 SWB-23 <0C> 80 Allowed 0000 Off    1  SeekDrive
       2 SWB-23 <0D> 80 Allowed 0000 Off    1  AltReset
       3 SWB-23 <11> 80 Blocked 0300 On     0  Recalibrate
       4 SWB-23 <47> 80 Blocked 0300 On     0  ExtendedSeek
     Results for SWB-23 category c on drive 80 Not all commands blocked (2
     of 5)
       0 SWB-23 <00> 81 Allowed 0000 Off    1  Reset
       1 SWB-23 <0C> 81 Allowed 0000 Off    1  SeekDrive
       2 SWB-23 <0D> 81 Allowed 0000 Off    1  AltReset
       3 SWB-23 <11> 81 Allowed 0000 Off    1  Recalibrate
       4 SWB-23 <47> 81 Allowed 0000 Off    1  ExtendedSeek
     Results for SWB-23 category c on drive 81 No commands blocked (0 of 5)
       0 SWB-23 <00> 82 Allowed 0000 Off    1  Reset
       1 SWB-23 <0C> 82 Allowed 0000 Off    1  SeekDrive
       2 SWB-23 <0D> 82 Allowed 0000 Off    1  AltReset
       3 SWB-23 <11> 82 Blocked 0300 On     0  Recalibrate
       4 SWB-23 <47> 82 Blocked 0300 On     0  ExtendedSeek
     Results for SWB-23 category c on drive 82 Not all commands blocked (2
     of 5)
       0 SWB-23 <00> 83 Allowed 0000 Off    1  Reset
       1 SWB-23 <0C> 83 Allowed 0000 Off    1  SeekDrive
       2 SWB-23 <0D> 83 Allowed 0000 Off    1  AltReset
       3 SWB-23 <11> 83 Blocked 0300 On     0  Recalibrate
       4 SWB-23 <47> 83 Blocked 0300 On     0  ExtendedSeek
     Results for SWB-23 category c on drive 83 Not all commands blocked (2
     of 5)
     Summary: 20 sent, 6 blocked, 14 not blocked
```

Results:

Assertion	Expected Results	Actual Results
AM-07	Tool active message	Tool active message
AM-08	4 drives identified	4 drives identified
AM-09	Drive 80 is protected	Drive 80 is protected
AM-09	Drive 81 is unprotected	Drive 81 is unprotected
AM-09	Drive 82 is protected	Drive 82 is protected
AM-09	Drive 83 is protected	Drive 83 is protected
AM-11	6 Commands return fail	6 Commands return fail
AO-05	No cmds to drive 80 blocked	Not all cmds to drive 80 blocked
AO-05	No cmds to drive 82 blocked	Not all cmds to drive 82 blocked
AO-05	No cmds to drive 83 blocked	Not all cmds to drive 83 blocked
AO-07	No cmds to drive 81 blocked	No cmds to drive 81 blocked

Analysis: SWB-23 Expected results not achieved for assertions: AO-05

Case Summary:	SWB-24 Install all drives, configure return code to success, protect with pattern even, execute control commands.
Assertions Tested:	SWB-AM-07. If the tool is executed then the tool shall issue a message indicating that the tool is active. SWB-AM-08. If the tool is executed then the tool shall issue a message indicating all drives accessible by the covered interfaces. SWB-AM-09. If the tool is executed then the tool shall issue a message indicating the protection status of each drive attached to a covered interface. SWB-AM-10. If the tool is configured to return success on blocked commands and the tool blocks a command then the return code shall indicate successful command execution. SWB-AO-05. If a subset of all covered drives is specified for protection, then commands from the control category shall not be blocked for drives in the selected subset. SWB-AO-07. If a subset of all covered drives is specified for protection, then no commands from any category shall be blocked for drives not in the selected subset.
Tester Name:	JRL
Test Date:	Sun Aug 31 09:18:25 2003
Test PC:	McMillan
Test Software:	SWBT 1.0
Hard Drives Used:	Drive 80, label F6 is an IBM-DTLA-307020 with 40188960 sectors Drive 81, label 6F is a Maxtor 6Y060L0 with 120103200 sectors Drive 82, label 64 is a WDC WD64AA with 12594960 sectors Drive 83, label E3 is a QUANTUM ATLAS10K2-TY092J with 17938985 sectors Drive 84, label 1F is a Quantum ATLAS10K3_18_SCA Drive with 35916548 sectors
Commands Executed:	Boot Test PC to (DOS 7.1) Windows 98 [Version 4.10.2222] tally13 hdl8 S024 test-hdl SWB-24 McMillan JRL c F6 6F 64 E3 1F Shutdown Test PC

Log File Highlights:	***** Monitor Execution *****
	Monitor BIOS interrupt 13h (disk service)
	tally13 compiled on 07/29/03 at 07:33:17
	@(#) Version 1.1 Created 07/29/03 at 07:28:05
	Now (08/31/03 at 09:18:17) Going . . . TSR
	***** Install HDL Log *****
	HDL -- Int_13 Hard Disk Write Lock V0.8 021126 (c)RCMP 1993-2002
	     ---- Royal Canadian Mounted Police ----
	     UNAUTHORIZED USE / DISTRIBUTION PROHIBITED
	
	     Licensee: US Dept. Commerce / NIST S/W Testing
	     5 Hard-Disks reported by Int_13h
	     Hard-Disk 0 Locked!
	     Hard-Disk 1 Not Locked!
	     Hard-Disk 2 Locked!
	     Hard-Disk 3 Not Locked!
	     Hard-Disk 4 Locked!
	     Write Lock successfully installed.
	***** Test Harness Log *****
	CMD: A:\TEST-HDL.EXE SWB-24 McMillan JRL c F6 6F 64 E3 1F
	Case: SWB-24
	Command set: Control
	Date: Sun Aug 31 09:18:25 2003
	
	Version: @(#) test-hdl.cpp Version 1.1 Created 08/23/03 at 10:13:51
	     @(#) wb-defs.h Version 1.2 Created 08/31/03 at 08:18:19
	     Compiled on Aug 31 2003 at 08:10:54
	Operator: JRL
	Host: McMillan
	Number of drives 5, Drives: F6 6F 64 E3 1F
	    Case Cmd Drv Action Stat Cry Count Cmd Name
	  0 SWB-24 <00> 80 Allowed 0000 Off 1 Reset
	  1 SWB-24 <0C> 80 Allowed 0000 Off 1 SeekDrive
	  2 SWB-24 <0D> 80 Allowed 0000 Off 1 AltReset
	  3 SWB-24 <11> 80 Blocked 0000 Off 0 Recalibrate
	  4 SWB-24 <47> 80 Blocked 0000 Off 0 ExtendedSeek
	Results for SWB-24 category c on drive 80 Not all commands blocked (2 of 5)
	  0 SWB-24 <00> 81 Allowed 0000 Off 1 Reset
	  1 SWB-24 <0C> 81 Allowed 0000 Off 1 SeekDrive

```
          2 SWB-24 <0D> 81 Allowed 0000 Off    1  AltReset
          3 SWB-24 <11> 81 Allowed 0000 Off    1  Recalibrate
          4 SWB-24 <47> 81 Allowed 0000 Off    1  ExtendedSeek
    Results for SWB-24 category c on drive 81 No commands blocked (0 of 5)
          0 SWB-24 <00> 82 Allowed 0000 Off    1  Reset
          1 SWB-24 <0C> 82 Allowed 0000 Off    1  SeekDrive
          2 SWB-24 <0D> 82 Allowed 0000 Off    1  AltReset
          3 SWB-24 <11> 82 Blocked 0000 Off    0  Recalibrate
          4 SWB-24 <47> 82 Blocked 0000 Off    0  ExtendedSeek
    Results for SWB-24 category c on drive 82 Not all commands blocked (2
    of 5)
          0 SWB-24 <00> 83 Allowed 0000 Off    1  Reset
          1 SWB-24 <0C> 83 Allowed 0000 Off    1  SeekDrive
          2 SWB-24 <0D> 83 Allowed 0000 Off    1  AltReset
          3 SWB-24 <11> 83 Allowed 0000 Off    1  Recalibrate
          4 SWB-24 <47> 83 Allowed 0000 Off    1  ExtendedSeek
    Results for SWB-24 category c on drive 83 No commands blocked (0 of 5)
          0 SWB-24 <00> 84 Allowed 0000 Off    1  Reset
          1 SWB-24 <0C> 84 Allowed 0000 Off    1  SeekDrive
          2 SWB-24 <0D> 84 Allowed 0000 Off    1  AltReset
          3 SWB-24 <11> 84 Blocked 0000 Off    0  Recalibrate
          4 SWB-24 <47> 84 Blocked 0000 Off    0  ExtendedSeek
    Results for SWB-24 category c on drive 84 Not all commands blocked (2
    of 5)
    Summary: 25 sent, 6 blocked, 19 not blocked
```

Results:

Assertion	Expected Results	Actual Results
AM-07	Tool active message	Tool active message
AM-08	5 drives identified	5 drives identified
AM-09	Drive 80 is protected	Drive 80 is protected
AM-09	Drive 81 is unprotected	Drive 81 is unprotected
AM-09	Drive 82 is protected	Drive 82 is protected
AM-09	Drive 83 is unprotected	Drive 83 is unprotected
AM-09	Drive 84 is protected	Drive 84 is protected
AM-10	6 Commands return success	6 Commands return success
AO-05	No cmds to drive 80 blocked	Not all cmds to drive 80 blocked
AO 05	No cmds to drive 82 blocked	Not all cmds to drive 82 blocked
AO-05	No cmds to drive 84 blocked	Not all cmds to drive 84 blocked
AO-07	No cmds to drive 81 blocked	No cmds to drive 81 blocked
AO-07	No cmds to drive 83 blocked	No cmds to drive 83 blocked

Analysis: SWB-24 Expected results not achieved for assertions: AO-05

Case SWB-25 HDL -- Int_13 Hard Disk Write Lock V0.8 021126 © RCMP 1993-2002	
Case Summary:	SWB-25 Install three drives, configure return code to failure, protect with pattern PUU, execute write commands.
Assertions Tested:	SWB-AM-07. If the tool is executed then the tool shall issue a message indicating that the tool is active. SWB-AM-08. If the tool is executed then the tool shall issue a message indicating all drives accessible by the covered interfaces. SWB-AM-09. If the tool is executed then the tool shall issue a message indicating the protection status of each drive attached to a covered interface. SWB-AM-11. If the tool is configured to return fail on blocked commands and the tool blocks a command then the return code shall indicate unsuccessful command execution. SWB-AO-01. If a subset of all covered drives is specified for protection, then commands from the write category shall be blocked for drives in the selected subset. SWB-AO-07. If a subset of all covered drives is specified for protection, then no commands from any category shall be blocked for drives not in the selected subset.
Tester Name:	JRL
Test Date:	Sun Aug 31 08:17:58 2003
Test PC:	Rumpole
Test Software:	SWBT 1.0

Case SWB-25 HDL -- Int_13 Hard Disk Write Lock V0.8 021126 © RCMP 1993-2002	
Hard Drives Used:	Drive 80, label 6F is a Maxtor 6Y060L0 with 120103200 sectors Drive 81, label 2B is a Quantum QM39100TD-SCA Drive with 17783249 sectors Drive 82, label 1F is a Quantum ATLAS10K3_18_SCA Drive with 35916548 sectors
Commands Executed:	Boot Test PC to (DOS 7.1) Windows 98 [Version 4.10.2222] tally13 hdl8 0 test-hdl SWB-25 Rumpole JRL w 6F 2B 1F Shutdown Test PC

Log File Highlights:	***** Monitor Execution *****
	Monitor BIOS interrupt 13h (disk service)
	tally13 compiled on 07/29/03 at 07:33:17
	@(#) Version 1.1 Created 07/29/03 at 07:28:05
	Now (08/31/03 at 08:17:55) Going . . . TSR
	***** Install HDL Log *****
	HDL -- Int_13 Hard Disk Write Lock V0.8 021126 (c)RCMP 1993-2002
	     ---- Royal Canadian Mounted Police ----
	     UNAUTHORIZED USE / DISTRIBUTION PROHIBITED
	
	     Licensee: US Dept. Commerce / NIST S/W Testing
	     3 Hard-Disks reported by Int_13h
	     Hard-Disk 0 Locked!
	     Hard-Disk 1 Not Locked!
	     Hard-Disk 2 Not Locked!
	     Write Lock successfully installed.
	***** Test Harness Log *****
	CMD: A:\TEST-HDL.EXE SWB-25 Rumpole JRL w 6F 2B 1F
	Case: SWB-25
	Command set: Write
	Date: Sun Aug 31 08:17:58 2003
	
	Version: @(#) test-hdl.cpp Version 1.1 Created 08/23/03 at 10:13:51
	     @(#) wb-defs.h Version 1.2 Created 08/31/03 at 08:18:19
	     Compiled on Aug 31 2003 at 08:10:54
	Operator: JRL
	Host: Rumpole
	Number of drives 3, Drives: 6F 2B 1F
	    Case Cmd Drv Action Stat Cry Count Cmd Name
	 0 SWB-25 <03> 80 Blocked 0300 On 0 WriteSectors
	 1 SWB-25 <0B> 80 Blocked 0300 On 0 WriteLong
	 2 SWB-25 <43> 80 Blocked 0300 On 0 ExtWrite
	Results for SWB-25 category w on drive 80 All commands blocked (3 of 3)
	 0 SWB-25 <03> 81 Allowed 0000 Off 1 WriteSectors
	 1 SWB-25 <0B> 81 Allowed 0000 Off 1 WriteLong
	 2 SWB-25 <43> 81 Allowed 0000 Off 1 ExtWrite
	Results for SWB-25 category w on drive 81 No commands blocked (0 of 3)
	 0 SWB-25 <03> 82 Allowed 0000 Off 1 WriteSectors
	 1 SWB-25 <0B> 82 Allowed 0000 Off 1 WriteLong
	 2 SWB-25 <43> 82 Allowed 0000 Off 1 ExtWrite
	Results for SWB-25 category w on drive 82 No commands blocked (0 of 3)
	Summary: 9 sent, 3 blocked, 6 not blocked

Results:	

Assertion	Expected Results	Actual Results
AM-07	Tool active message	Tool active message
AM-08	3 drives identified	3 drives identified
AM-09	Drive 80 is protected	Drive 80 is protected
AM-09	Drive 81 is unprotected	Drive 81 is unprotected
AM-09	Drive 82 is unprotected	Drive 82 is unprotected
AM-11	3 Commands return fail	3 Commands return fail
AO-01	All cmds to drive 80 blocked	All cmds to drive 80 blocked
AO-07	No cmds to drive 81 blocked	No cmds to drive 81 blocked
AO-07	No cmds to drive 82 blocked	No cmds to drive 82 blocked

Analysis:	SWB-25 Expected results achieved

Case SWB-26 HDL -- Int_13 Hard Disk Write Lock V0.8 021126 © RCMP 1993-2002	
Case Summary:	SWB-26 Install three drives, configure return code to success, protect

	with pattern UPU, execute write commands.
Assertions Tested:	SWB-AM-07. If the tool is executed then the tool shall issue a message indicating that the tool is active. SWB-AM-08. If the tool is executed then the tool shall issue a message indicating all drives accessible by the covered interfaces. SWB-AM-09. If the tool is executed then the tool shall issue a message indicating the protection status of each drive attached to a covered interface. SWB-AM-10. If the tool is configured to return success on blocked commands and the tool blocks a command then the return code shall indicate successful command execution. SWB-AO-01. If a subset of all covered drives is specified for protection, then commands from the write category shall be blocked for drives in the selected subset. SWB-AO-07. If a subset of all covered drives is specified for protection, then no commands from any category shall be blocked for drives not in the selected subset.
Tester Name:	JRL
Test Date:	Sun Aug 31 09:09:04 2003
Test PC:	Wimsey
Test Software:	SWBT 1.0
Hard Drives Used:	Drive 80, label 90 is a WDC WD300BB-00CAA0 with 58633344 sectors Drive 81, label 64 is a WDC WD64AA with 12594960 sectors Drive 82, label E3 is a QUANTUM ATLAS10K2-TY092J with 17938985 sectors
Commands Executed:	Boot Test PC to (DOS 7.1) Windows 98 [Version 4.10.2222] tally13 hdl8 S1 test-hdl SWB-26 Wimsey JRL w 90 64 E3 Shutdown Test PC

Log File Highlights:	***** Monitor Execution *****
	Monitor BIOS interrupt 13h (disk service)
	tally13 compiled on 07/29/03 at 07:33:17
	@(#) Version 1.1 Created 07/29/03 at 07:28:05
	Now (08/31/03 at 09:09:02) Going . . . TSR
	***** Install HDL Log *****
	HDL -- Int_13 Hard Disk Write Lock V0.8 021126 (c)RCMP 1993-2002
	    ---- Royal Canadian Mounted Police ----
	    UNAUTHORIZED USE / DISTRIBUTION PROHIBITED
	
	    Licensee: US Dept. Commerce / NIST S/W Testing
	    3 Hard-Disks reported by Int_13h
	    Hard-Disk 0 Not Locked!
	    Hard-Disk 1 Locked!
	    Hard-Disk 2 Not Locked!
	    Write Lock successfully installed.
	***** Test Harness Log *****
	CMD: A:\TEST-HDL.EXE SWB-26 Wimsey JRL w 90 64 E3
	Case: SWB-26
	Command set: Write
	Date: Sun Aug 31 09:09:04 2003
	
	Version: @(#) test-hdl.cpp Version 1.1 Created 08/23/03 at 10:13:51
	    @(#) wb-defs.h Version 1.2 Created 08/31/03 at 08:18:19
	    Compiled on Aug 31 2003 at 08:10:54
	Operator: JRL
	Host: Wimsey
	Number of drives 3, Drives: 90 64 E3
	    Case Cmd Drv Action Stat Cry Count Cmd Name
	  0 SWB-26 <03> 80 Allowed 0000 Off 1 WriteSectors
	  1 SWB-26 <0B> 80 Allowed 0000 Off 1 WriteLong
	  2 SWB-26 <43> 80 Allowed 0000 Off 1 ExtWrite
	Results for SWB-26 category w on drive 80 No commands blocked (0 of 3)
	  0 SWB-26 <03> 81 Blocked 0000 Off 0 WriteSectors
	  1 SWB-26 <0B> 81 Blocked 0000 Off 0 WriteLong
	  2 SWB-26 <43> 81 Blocked 0000 Off 0 ExtWrite
	Results for SWB-26 category w on drive 81 All commands blocked (3 of 3)
	  0 SWB-26 <03> 82 Allowed 0000 Off 1 WriteSectors
	  1 SWB-26 <0B> 82 Allowed 0000 Off 1 WriteLong
	  2 SWB-26 <43> 82 Allowed 0000 Off 1 ExtWrite
	Results for SWB-26 category w on drive 82 No commands blocked (0 of 3)
	Summary: 9 sent, 3 blocked, 6 not blocked

Case SWB-26 HDL -- Int_13 Hard Disk Write Lock V0.8 021126 © RCMP 1993-2002

Results:

Assertion	Expected Results	Actual Results
AM-07	Tool active message	Tool active message
AM-08	3 drives identified	3 drives identified
AM-09	Drive 80 is unprotected	Drive 80 is unprotected
AM-09	Drive 81 is protected	Drive 81 is protected
AM-09	Drive 82 is unprotected	Drive 82 is unprotected
AM-10	3 Commands return success	3 Commands return success
AO-01	All cmds to drive 81 blocked	All cmds to drive 81 blocked
AO-07	No cmds to drive 80 blocked	No cmds to drive 80 blocked
AO-07	No cmds to drive 82 blocked	No cmds to drive 82 blocked

Analysis: | SWB-26 Expected results achieved

Case SWB-27 HDL -- Int_13 Hard Disk Write Lock V0.8 021126 © RCMP 1993-2002

Case Summary:	SWB-27 Install three drives, configure return code to failure, protect with pattern UUP, execute write commands.
Assertions Tested:	SWB-AM-07. If the tool is executed then the tool shall issue a message indicating that the tool is active. SWB-AM-08. If the tool is executed then the tool shall issue a message indicating all drives accessible by the covered interfaces. SWB-AM-09. If the tool is executed then the tool shall issue a message indicating the protection status of each drive attached to a covered interface. SWB-AM-11. If the tool is configured to return fail on blocked commands and the tool blocks a command then the return code shall indicate unsuccessful command execution. SWB-AO-01. If a subset of all covered drives is specified for protection, then commands from the write category shall be blocked for drives in the selected subset. SWB-AO-07. If a subset of all covered drives is specified for protection, then no commands from any category shall be blocked for drives not in the selected subset.
Tester Name:	JRL
Test Date:	Sun Aug 31 09:16:57 2003
Test PC:	McCloud
Test Software:	SWBT 1.0
Hard Drives Used:	Drive 80, label 8A is a WDC WD200EB-00CSF0 with 39102336 sectors Drive 81, label F5 is an IBM-DTLA-307020 with 40188960 sectors Drive 82, label F6 is an IBM-DTLA-307020 with 40188960 sectors
Commands Executed:	Boot Test PC to (DOS 7.1) Windows 98 [Version 4.10.2222] tally13 hdl8 2 test-hdl SWB-27 McCloud JRL w 8A F5 F6 Shutdown Test PC

Log File Highlights:	***** Monitor Execution *****
	Monitor BIOS interrupt 13h (disk service)
	tally13 compiled on 07/29/03 at 07:33:17
	@(#) Version 1.1 Created 07/29/03 at 07:28:05
	Now (08/31/03 at 09:16:50) Going . . . TSR
	***** Install HDL Log *****
	HDL -- Int_13 Hard Disk Write Lock V0.8 021126 (c)RCMP 1993-2002
	    ---- Royal Canadian Mounted Police ----
	    UNAUTHORIZED USE / DISTRIBUTION PROHIBITED
	
	    Licensee: US Dept. Commerce / NIST S/W Testing
	    3 Hard-Disks reported by Int_13h
	    Hard-Disk 0 Not Locked!
	    Hard-Disk 1 Not Locked!
	    Hard-Disk 2 Locked!
	    Write Lock successfully installed.
	***** Test Harness Log *****
	CMD: A:\TEST-HDL.EXE SWB-27 McCloud JRL w 8A F5 F6
	Case: SWB-27
	Command set: Write
	Date: Sun Aug 31 09:16:57 2003
	
	Version: @(#) test-hdl.cpp Version 1.1 Created 08/23/03 at 10:13:51
	    @(#) wb-defs.h Version 1.2 Created 08/31/03 at 08:18:19
	    Compiled on Aug 31 2003 at 08:10:54

	Operator: JRL
	Host: McCloud
	Number of drives 3, Drives: 8A F5 F6
	      Case Cmd Drv Action Stat Cry Count Cmd Name
	  0 SWB-27 \<03\> 80 Allowed 0000 Off 1 WriteSectors
	  1 SWB-27 \<0B\> 80 Allowed 0000 Off 1 WriteLong
	  2 SWB-27 \<43\> 80 Allowed 0000 Off 1 ExtWrite
	Results for SWB-27 category w on drive 80 No commands blocked (0 of 3)
	  0 SWB-27 \<03\> 81 Allowed 0000 Off 1 WriteSectors
	  1 SWB-27 \<0B\> 81 Allowed 0000 Off 1 WriteLong
	  2 SWB-27 \<43\> 81 Allowed 0000 Off 1 ExtWrite
	Results for SWB-27 category w on drive 81 No commands blocked (0 of 3)
	  0 SWB-27 \<03\> 82 Blocked 0300 On 0 WriteSectors
	  1 SWB-27 \<0B\> 82 Blocked 0300 On 0 WriteLong
	  2 SWB-27 \<43\> 82 Blocked 0300 On 0 ExtWrite
	Results for SWB-27 category w on drive 82 All commands blocked (3 of 3)
	Summary: 9 sent, 3 blocked, 6 not blocked

Results:			
	Assertion	**Expected Results**	**Actual Results**
	AM-07	Tool active message	Tool active message
	AM-08	3 drives identified	3 drives identified
	AM-09	Drive 80 is unprotected	Drive 80 is unprotected
	AM-09	Drive 81 is unprotected	Drive 81 is unprotected
	AM-09	Drive 82 is protected	Drive 82 is protected
	AM-11	3 Commands return fail	3 Commands return fail
	AO-01	All cmds to drive 82 blocked	All cmds to drive 82 blocked
	AO-07	No cmds to drive 80 blocked	No cmds to drive 80 blocked
	AO-07	No cmds to drive 81 blocked	No cmds to drive 81 blocked

Analysis:	SWB-27 Expected results achieved

Case Summary:	SWB-28 Install three drives, configure return code to success, protect with pattern UPP, execute write commands.
Assertions Tested:	SWB-AM-07. If the tool is executed then the tool shall issue a message indicating that the tool is active. SWB-AM-08. If the tool is executed then the tool shall issue a message indicating all drives accessible by the covered interfaces. SWB-AM-09. If the tool is executed then the tool shall issue a message indicating the protection status of each drive attached to a covered interface. SWB-AM-10. If the tool is configured to return success on blocked commands and the tool blocks a command then the return code shall indicate successful command execution. SWB-AO-01. If a subset of all covered drives is specified for protection, then commands from the write category shall be blocked for drives in the selected subset. SWB-AO-07. If a subset of all covered drives is specified for protection, then no commands from any category shall be blocked for drives not in the selected subset.
Tester Name:	JRL
Test Date:	Sun Aug 31 08:20:42 2003
Test PC:	Rumpole
Test Software:	SWBT 1.0
Hard Drives Used:	Drive 80, label 6F is a Maxtor 6Y060L0 with 120103200 sectors Drive 81, label 2B is a Quantum QM39100TD-SCA Drive with 17783249 sectors Drive 82, label 1F is a Quantum ATLAS10K3_18_SCA Drive with 35916548 sectors
Commands Executed:	Boot Test PC to (DOS 7.1) Windows 98 [Version 4.10.2222] tally13 hdl8 S12 test-hdl SWB-28 Rumpole JRL w 6F 2B 1F Shutdown Test PC
Log File Highlights:	***** Monitor Execution ***** Monitor BIOS interrupt 13h (disk service) tally13 compiled on 07/29/03 at 07:33:17 @(#) Version 1.1 Created 07/29/03 at 07:28:05

```
                Now (08/31/03 at 08:20:40) Going . . .   TSR
                ***** Install HDL Log *****
                HDL -- Int_13 Hard Disk Write Lock V0.8 021126 (c)RCMP 1993-2002
                     ---- Royal Canadian Mounted Police ----
                     UNAUTHORIZED USE / DISTRIBUTION PROHIBITED

                     Licensee: US Dept. Commerce / NIST S/W Testing
                     3 Hard-Disks reported by Int_13h
                     Hard-Disk 0 Not Locked!
                     Hard-Disk 1    Locked!
                     Hard-Disk 2    Locked!
                     Write Lock successfully installed.
                ***** Test Harness Log *****
                CMD: A:\TEST-HDL.EXE SWB-28 Rumpole JRL w 6F 2B 1F
                Case: SWB-28
                Command set: Write
                Date: Sun Aug 31 08:20:42 2003

                Version: @(#) test-hdl.cpp Version 1.1 Created 08/23/03 at 10:13:51
                        @(#) wb-defs.h Version 1.2 Created 08/31/03 at 08:18:19
                        Compiled on Aug 31 2003 at 08:10:54
                Operator: JRL
                Host: Rumpole
                Number of drives 3, Drives: 6F 2B 1F
                    Case  Cmd Drv Action  Stat Cry Count Cmd Name
                 0  SWB-28 <03> 80 Allowed 0000 Off     1  WriteSectors
                 1  SWB-28 <0B> 80 Allowed 0000 Off     1  WriteLong
                 2  SWB-28 <43> 80 Allowed 0000 Off     1  ExtWrite
                Results for SWB-28 category w on drive 80 No commands blocked (0 of 3)
                 0  SWB-28 <03> 81 Blocked 0000 Off     0  WriteSectors
                 1  SWB-28 <0B> 81 Blocked 0000 Off     0  WriteLong
                 2  SWB-28 <43> 81 Blocked 0000 Off     0  ExtWrite
                Results for SWB-28 category w on drive 81 All commands blocked (3 of 3)
                 0  SWB-28 <03> 82 Blocked 0000 Off     0  WriteSectors
                 1  SWB-28 <0B> 82 Blocked 0000 Off     0  WriteLong
                 2  SWB-28 <43> 82 Blocked 0000 Off     0  ExtWrite
                Results for SWB-28 category w on drive 82 All commands blocked (3 of 3)
                Summary: 9 sent, 6 blocked, 3 not blocked
```

Results:			
	Assertion	**Expected Results**	**Actual Results**
	AM-07	Tool active message	Tool active message
	AM-08	3 drives identified	3 drives identified
	AM-09	Drive 80 is unprotected	Drive 80 is unprotected
	AM-09	Drive 81 is protected	Drive 81 is protected
	AM-09	Drive 82 is protected	Drive 82 is protected
	AM-10	6 Commands return fail	6 Commands return fail
	AO-01	All cmds to drive 81 blocked	All cmds to drive 81 blocked
	AO-01	All cmds to drive 82 blocked	All cmds to drive 82 blocked
	AO-07	No cmds to drive 80 blocked	No cmds to drive 80 blocked

Analysis:	SWB-28 Expected results achieved

Case Summary:	SWB-29 Install three drives, configure return code to failure, protect with pattern PUP, execute write commands.
Assertions Tested:	SWB-AM-07. If the tool is executed then the tool shall issue a message indicating that the tool is active.
	SWB-AM-08. If the tool is executed then the tool shall issue a message indicating all drives accessible by the covered interfaces.
	SWB-AM-09. If the tool is executed then the tool shall issue a message indicating the protection status of each drive attached to a covered interface.
	SWB-AM-11. If the tool is configured to return fail on blocked commands and the tool blocks a command then the return code shall indicate unsuccessful command execution.
	SWB-AO-01. If a subset of all covered drives is specified for protection, then commands from the write category shall be blocked for drives in the selected subset.

Case SWB-29 HDL -- Int_13 Hard Disk Write Lock V0.8 021126 © RCMP 1993-2002	
	SWB-AO-07. If a subset of all covered drives is specified for protection, then no commands from any category shall be blocked for drives not in the selected subset.
Tester Name:	JRL
Test Date:	Sun Aug 31 09:12:16 2003
Test PC:	Wimsey
Test Software:	SWBT 1.0
Hard Drives Used:	Drive 80, label 90 is a WDC WD300BB-00CAA0 with 58633344 sectors Drive 81, label 64 is a WDC WD64AA with 12594960 sectors Drive 82, label E3 is a QUANTUM ATLAS10K2-TY092J with 17938985 sectors
Commands Executed:	Boot Test PC to (DOS 7.1) Windows 98 [Version 4.10.2222] tally13 hdl8 02 test-hdl SWB-29 Wimsey JRL w 90 64 E3 Shutdown Test PC

Log File Highlights:	***** Monitor Execution *****
	Monitor BIOS interrupt 13h (disk service)
	tally13 compiled on 07/29/03 at 07:33:17
	@(#) Version 1.1 Created 07/29/03 at 07:28:05
	Now (08/31/03 at 09:12:13) Going . . . TSR
	***** Install HDL Log *****
	HDL -- Int_13 Hard Disk Write Lock V0.8 021126 (c)RCMP 1993-2002
	    ---- Royal Canadian Mounted Police ----
	    UNAUTHORIZED USE / DISTRIBUTION PROHIBITED
	
	    Licensee: US Dept. Commerce / NIST S/W Testing
	    3 Hard-Disks reported by Int_13h
	    Hard-Disk 0 Locked!
	    Hard-Disk 1 Not Locked!
	    Hard-Disk 2 Locked!
	    Write Lock successfully installed.
	***** Test Harness Log *****
	CMD: A:\TEST-HDL.EXE SWB-29 Wimsey JRL w 90 64 E3
	Case: SWB-29
	Command set: Write
	Date: Sun Aug 31 09:12:16 2003
	
	Version: @(#) test-hdl.cpp Version 1.1 Created 08/23/03 at 10:13:51
	    @(#) wb-defs.h Version 1.2 Created 08/31/03 at 08:18:19
	    Compiled on Aug 31 2003 at 08:10:54
	Operator: JRL
	Host: Wimsey
	Number of drives 3, Drives: 90 64 E3
	    Case Cmd Drv Action Stat Cry Count Cmd Name
	 0 SWB-29 <03> 80 Blocked 0300 On 0 WriteSectors
	 1 SWB-29 <0B> 80 Blocked 0300 On 0 WriteLong
	 2 SWB-29 <43> 80 Blocked 0300 On 0 ExtWrite
	Results for SWB-29 category w on drive 80 All commands blocked (3 of 3)
	 0 SWB-29 <03> 81 Allowed 0000 Off 1 WriteSectors
	 1 SWB-29 <0B> 81 Allowed 0000 Off 1 WriteLong
	 2 SWB-29 <43> 81 Allowed 0000 Off 1 ExtWrite
	Results for SWB-29 category w on drive 81 No commands blocked (0 of 3)
	 0 SWB-29 <03> 82 Blocked 0300 On 0 WriteSectors
	 1 SWB-29 <0B> 82 Blocked 0300 On 0 WriteLong
	 2 SWB-29 <43> 82 Blocked 0300 On 0 ExtWrite
	Results for SWB-29 category w on drive 82 All commands blocked (3 of 3)
	Summary: 9 sent, 6 blocked, 3 not blocked

Results:			
	Assertion	**Expected Results**	**Actual Results**
	AM-07	Tool active message	Tool active message
	AM-08	3 drives identified	3 drives identified
	AM-09	Drive 80 is protected	Drive 80 is protected
	AM-09	Drive 81 is unprotected	Drive 81 is unprotected
	AM-09	Drive 82 is protected	Drive 82 is protected
	AM-11	6 Commands return fail	6 Commands return fail
	AO-01	All cmds to drive 80 blocked	All cmds to drive 80 blocked
	AO-01	All cmds to drive 82 blocked	All cmds to drive 82 blocked
	AO-07	No cmds to drive 81 blocked	No cmds to drive 81 blocked

Analysis:	SWB-29 Expected results achieved

Case SWB-30 HDL -- Int_13 Hard Disk Write Lock V0.8 021126 © RCMP 1993-2002	
Case Summary:	SWB-30 Install three drives, configure return code to success, protect with pattern PPU, execute write commands.
Assertions Tested:	SWB-AM-07. If the tool is executed then the tool shall issue a message indicating that the tool is active. SWB-AM-08. If the tool is executed then the tool shall issue a message indicating all drives accessible by the covered interfaces. SWB-AM-09. If the tool is executed then the tool shall issue a message indicating the protection status of each drive attached to a covered interface. SWB-AM-10. If the tool is configured to return success on blocked commands and the tool blocks a command then the return code shall indicate successful command execution. SWB-AO-01. If a subset of all covered drives is specified for protection, then commands from the write category shall be blocked for drives in the selected subset. SWB-AO-07. If a subset of all covered drives is specified for protection, then no commands from any category shall be blocked for drives not in the selected subset.
Tester Name:	JRL
Test Date:	Sun Aug 31 08:24:15 2003
Test PC:	Rumpole
Test Software:	SWBT 1.0
Hard Drives Used:	Drive 80, label 6F is a Maxtor 6Y060L0 with 120103200 sectors Drive 81, label 2B is a Quantum QM39100TD-SCA Drive with 17783249 sectors Drive 82, label 1F is a Quantum ATLAS10K3_18_SCA Drive with 35916548 sectors
Commands Executed:	Boot Test PC to (DOS 7.1) Windows 98 [Version 4.10.2222] tally13 hdl8 S01 test-hdl SWB-30 Rumpole JRL w 6F 2B 1F Shutdown Test PC

Log File Highlights:	***** Monitor Execution *****
	Monitor BIOS interrupt 13h (disk service)
	tally13 compiled on 07/29/03 at 07:33:17
	@(#) Version 1.1 Created 07/29/03 at 07:28:05
	Now (08/31/03 at 08:24:10) Going . . . TSR
	***** Install HDL Log *****
	HDL -- Int_13 Hard Disk Write Lock V0.8 021126 (c)RCMP 1993-2002
	    ---- Royal Canadian Mounted Police ----
	    UNAUTHORIZED USE / DISTRIBUTION PROHIBITED
	
	    Licensee: US Dept. Commerce / NIST S/W Testing
	    3 Hard-Disks reported by Int_13h
	    Hard-Disk 0 Locked!
	    Hard-Disk 1 Locked!
	    Hard-Disk 2 Not Locked!
	    Write Lock successfully installed.
	***** Test Harness Log *****
	CMD: A:\TEST-HDL.EXE SWB-30 Rumpole JRL w 6F 2B 1F
	Case: SWB-30
	Command set: Write
	Date: Sun Aug 31 08:24:15 2003
	
	Version: @(#) test-hdl.cpp Version 1.1 Created 08/23/03 at 10:13:51
	    @(#) wb-defs.h Version 1.2 Created 08/31/03 at 08:18:19
	    Compiled on Aug 31 2003 at 08:10:54
	Operator: JRL
	Host: Rumpole
	Number of drives 3, Drives: 6F 2B 1F
	    Case Cmd Drv Action Stat Cry Count Cmd Name
	  0 SWB-30 <03> 80 Blocked 0000 Off 0 WriteSectors
	  1 SWB-30 <0B> 80 Blocked 0000 Off 0 WriteLong
	  2 SWB-30 <43> 80 Blocked 0000 Off 0 ExtWrite
	Results for SWB-30 category w on drive 80 All commands blocked (3 of 3)
	  0 SWB-30 <03> 81 Blocked 0000 Off 0 WriteSectors
	  1 SWB-30 <0B> 81 Blocked 0000 Off 0 WriteLong
	  2 SWB-30 <43> 81 Blocked 0000 Off 0 ExtWrite

	Results for SWB-30 category w on drive 81 All commands blocked (3 of 3)
	  0 SWB-30 <03> 82 Allowed 0000 Off 1 WriteSectors
	  1 SWB-30 <0B> 82 Allowed 0000 Off 1 WriteLong
	  2 SWB-30 <43> 82 Allowed 0000 Off 1 ExtWrite
	Results for SWB-30 category w on drive 82 No commands blocked (0 of 3)
	Summary: 9 sent, 6 blocked, 3 not blocked

Results:			
	Assertion	**Expected Results**	**Actual Results**
	AM-07	Tool active message	Tool active message
	AM-08	3 drives identified	3 drives identified
	AM-09	Drive 80 is protected	Drive 80 is protected
	AM-09	Drive 81 is protected	Drive 81 is protected
	AM-09	Drive 82 is unprotected	Drive 82 is unprotected
	AM-10	6 Commands return success	6 Commands return success
	AO-01	All cmds to drive 80 blocked	All cmds to drive 80 blocked
	AO-01	All cmds to drive 81 blocked	All cmds to drive 81 blocked
	AO-07	No cmds to drive 82 blocked	No cmds to drive 82 blocked

Analysis:	SWB-30 Expected results achieved

Case Summary:	SWB-31 Install three drives, configure return code to failure, protect with pattern PUU, execute read commands.
Assertions Tested:	SWB-AM-07. If the tool is executed then the tool shall issue a message indicating that the tool is active. SWB-AM-08. If the tool is executed then the tool shall issue a message indicating all drives accessible by the covered interfaces. SWB-AM-09. If the tool is executed then the tool shall issue a message indicating the protection status of each drive attached to a covered interface. SWB-AM-11. If the tool is configured to return fail on blocked commands and the tool blocks a command then the return code shall indicate unsuccessful command execution. SWB-AO-04. If a subset of all covered drives is specified for protection, then commands from the read category shall not be blocked for drives in the selected subset. SWB-AO-07. If a subset of all covered drives is specified for protection, then no commands from any category shall be blocked for drives not in the selected subset.
Tester Name:	JRL
Test Date:	Sun Aug 31 09:21:35 2003
Test PC:	McCloud
Test Software:	SWBT 1.0
Hard Drives Used:	Drive 80, label 8A is a WDC WD200EB-00CSF0 with 39102336 sectors Drive 81, label F5 is an IBM-DTLA-307020 with 40188960 sectors Drive 82, label F6 is an IBM-DTLA-307020 with 40188960 sectors
Commands Executed:	Boot Test PC to (DOS 7.1) Windows 98 [Version 4.10.2222] tally13 hdl8 0 test-hdl SWB-31 McCloud JRL r 8A F5 F6 Shutdown Test PC

Log File Highlights:	***** Monitor Execution *****
	Monitor BIOS interrupt 13h (disk service)
	tally13 compiled on 07/29/03 at 07:33:17
	@(#) Version 1.1 Created 07/29/03 at 07:28:05
	Now (08/31/03 at 09:21:28) Going . . . TSR
	***** Install HDL Log *****
	HDL -- Int_13 Hard Disk Write Lock V0.8 021126 (c)RCMP 1993-2002
	    ---- Royal Canadian Mounted Police ----
	    UNAUTHORIZED USE / DISTRIBUTION PROHIBITED
	
	    Licensee: US Dept. Commerce / NIST S/W Testing
	    3 Hard-Disks reported by Int_13h
	    Hard-Disk 0 Locked!
	    Hard-Disk 1 Not Locked!
	    Hard-Disk 2 Not Locked!
	    Write Lock successfully installed.

Case SWB-31 HDL -- Int_13 Hard Disk Write Lock V0.8 021126 © RCMP 1993-2002

```
***** Test Harness Log *****
CMD: A:\TEST-HDL.EXE SWB-31 McCloud JRL r 8A F5 F6
Case: SWB-31
Command set: Read
Date: Sun Aug 31 09:21:35 2003

Version: @(#) test-hdl.cpp Version 1.1 Created 08/23/03 at 10:13:51
         @(#) wb-defs.h Version 1.2 Created 08/31/03 at 08:18:19
         Compiled on Aug 31 2003 at 08:10:54
Operator: JRL
Host: McCloud
Number of drives 3, Drives: 8A F5 F6
      Case  Cmd Drv Action  Stat Cry Count Cmd Name
   0 SWB-31 <02> 80 Allowed 0000 Off     1 ReadSectors
   1 SWB-31 <0A> 80 Allowed 0000 Off     1 ReadLong
   2 SWB-31 <42> 80 Allowed 0000 Off     1 ExtRead
Results for SWB-31 category r on drive 80 No commands blocked (0 of 3)
   0 SWB-31 <02> 81 Allowed 0000 Off     1 ReadSectors
   1 SWB-31 <0A> 81 Allowed 0000 Off     1 ReadLong
   2 SWB-31 <42> 81 Allowed 0000 Off     1 ExtRead
Results for SWB-31 category r on drive 81 No commands blocked (0 of 3)
   0 SWB-31 <02> 82 Allowed 0000 Off     1 ReadSectors
   1 SWB-31 <0A> 82 Allowed 0000 Off     1 ReadLong
   2 SWB-31 <42> 82 Allowed 0000 Off     1 ExtRead
Results for SWB-31 category r on drive 82 No commands blocked (0 of 3)
Summary: 9 sent, 0 blocked, 9 not blocked
```

Results:			

Assertion	Expected Results	Actual Results
AM-07	Tool active message	Tool active message
AM-08	3 drives identified	3 drives identified
AM-09	Drive 80 is protected	Drive 80 is protected
AM-09	Drive 81 is unprotected	Drive 81 is unprotected
AM-09	Drive 82 is unprotected	Drive 82 is unprotected
AM-11	0 Commands return fail	0 Commands return fail
AO-04	No cmds to drive 80 blocked	No cmds to drive 80 blocked
AO-07	No cmds to drive 81 blocked	No cmds to drive 81 blocked
AO-07	No cmds to drive 82 blocked	No cmds to drive 82 blocked

Analysis:	SWB-31 Expected results achieved

Case SWB-32 HDL -- Int_13 Hard Disk Write Lock V0.8 021126 © RCMP 1993-2002

Case Summary:	SWB-32 Install three drives, configure return code to success, protect with pattern UPU, execute read commands.
Assertions Tested:	SWB-AM-07. If the tool is executed then the tool shall issue a message indicating that the tool is active. SWB-AM-08. If the tool is executed then the tool shall issue a message indicating all drives accessible by the covered interfaces. SWB-AM-09. If the tool is executed then the tool shall issue a message indicating the protection status of each drive attached to a covered interface. SWB-AM-10. If the tool is configured to return success on blocked commands and the tool blocks a command then the return code shall indicate successful command execution. SWB-AO-04. If a subset of all covered drives is specified for protection, then commands from the read category shall not be blocked for drives in the selected subset. SWB-AO-07. If a subset of all covered drives is specified for protection, then no commands from any category shall be blocked for drives not in the selected subset.
Tester Name:	JRL
Test Date:	Sun Aug 31 09:15:59 2003
Test PC:	Wimsey
Test Software:	SWBT 1.0
Hard Drives Used:	Drive 80, label 90 is a WDC WD300BB-00CAA0 with 58633344 sectors Drive 81, label 64 is a WDC WD64AA with 12594960 sectors Drive 82, label E3 is a QUANTUM ATLAS10K2-TY092J with 17938985 sectors
Commands Executed:	Boot Test PC to (DOS 7.1) Windows 98 [Version 4.10.2222] tally13 hdl8 S1

	Case SWB-32 HDL -- Int_13 Hard Disk Write Lock V0.8 021126 © RCMP 1993-2002
	test-hdl SWB-32 Wimsey JRL r 90 64 E3 Shutdown Test PC

Log File
Highlights:
	***** Monitor Execution *****
	Monitor BIOS interrupt 13h (disk service)
	tally13 compiled on 07/29/03 at 07:33:17
	@(#) Version 1.1 Created 07/29/03 at 07:28:05
	Now (08/31/03 at 09:15:56) Going . . . TSR
	***** Install HDL Log *****
	HDL -- Int_13 Hard Disk Write Lock V0.8 021126 (c)RCMP 1993-2002
	    ---- Royal Canadian Mounted Police ----
	    UNAUTHORIZED USE / DISTRIBUTION PROHIBITED
	
	    Licensee: US Dept. Commerce / NIST S/W Testing
	    3 Hard-Disks reported by Int_13h
	    Hard-Disk 0 Not Locked!
	    Hard-Disk 1 Locked!
	    Hard-Disk 2 Not Locked!
	    Write Lock successfully installed.
	***** Test Harness Log *****
	CMD: A:\TEST-HDL.EXE SWB-32 Wimsey JRL r 90 64 E3
	Case: SWB-32
	Command set: Read
	Date: Sun Aug 31 09:15:59 2003
	
	Version: @(#) test-hdl.cpp Version 1.1 Created 08/23/03 at 10:13:51
	    @(#) wb-defs.h Version 1.2 Created 08/31/03 at 08:18:19
	    Compiled on Aug 31 2003 at 08:10:54
	Operator: JRL
	Host: Wimsey
	Number of drives 3, Drives: 90 64 E3
	    Case Cmd Drv Action Stat Cry Count Cmd Name
	 0 SWB-32 <02> 80 Allowed 0000 Off 1 ReadSectors
	 1 SWB-32 <0A> 80 Allowed 0000 Off 1 ReadLong
	 2 SWB-32 <42> 80 Allowed 0000 Off 1 ExtRead
	Results for SWB-32 category r on drive 80 No commands blocked (0 of 3)
	 0 SWB-32 <02> 81 Allowed 0000 Off 1 ReadSectors
	 1 SWB-32 <0A> 81 Allowed 0000 Off 1 ReadLong
	 2 SWB-32 <42> 81 Allowed 0000 Off 1 ExtRead
	Results for SWB-32 category r on drive 81 No commands blocked (0 of 3)
	 0 SWB-32 <02> 82 Allowed 0000 Off 1 ReadSectors
	 1 SWB-32 <0A> 82 Allowed 0000 Off 1 ReadLong
	 2 SWB-32 <42> 82 Allowed 0000 Off 1 ExtRead
	Results for SWB-32 category r on drive 82 No commands blocked (0 of 3)
	Summary: 9 sent, 0 blocked, 9 not blocked

Results:

Assertion	Expected Results	Actual Results
AM-07	Tool active message	Tool active message
AM-08	3 drives identified	3 drives identified
AM-09	Drive 80 is unprotected	Drive 80 is unprotected
AM-09	Drive 81 is protected	Drive 81 is protected
AM-09	Drive 82 is unprotected	Drive 82 is unprotected
AM-10	0 Commands return success	0 Commands return success
AO-04	No cmds to drive 81 blocked	No cmds to drive 81 blocked
AO-07	No cmds to drive 80 blocked	No cmds to drive 80 blocked
AO-07	No cmds to drive 82 blocked	No cmds to drive 82 blocked

Analysis:	SWB-32 Expected results achieved

	Case SWB-33 HDL -- Int_13 Hard Disk Write Lock V0.8 021126 © RCMP 1993-2002
Case Summary:	SWB-33 Install three drives, configure return code to failure, protect with pattern UUP, execute read commands.

Assertions
Tested:
	SWB-AM-07. If the tool is executed then the tool shall issue a message
	    indicating that the tool is active.
	SWB-AM-08. If the tool is executed then the tool shall issue a message
	    indicating all drives accessible by the covered interfaces.
	SWB-AM-09. If the tool is executed then the tool shall issue a message
	    indicating the protection status of each drive attached to a
	    covered interface.
	SWB-AM-11. If the tool is configured to return fail on blocked commands

	and the tool blocks a command then the return code shall indicate unsuccessful command execution. SWB-AO-04. If a subset of all covered drives is specified for protection, then commands from the read category shall not be blocked for drives in the selected subset. SWB-AO-07. If a subset of all covered drives is specified for protection, then no commands from any category shall be blocked for drives not in the selected subset.
Tester Name:	JRL
Test Date:	Sun Aug 31 08:26:26 2003
Test PC:	Rumpole
Test Software:	SWBT 1.0
Hard Drives Used:	Drive 80, label 6F is a Maxtor 6□060L0 with 120103200 sectors Drive 81, label 2B is a □uantum □M39100TD-SCA Drive with 17783249 sectors Drive 82, label 1F is a □uantum ATLAS10□3_18_SCA Drive with 35916548 sectors
Commands Executed:	Boot Test PC to (DOS 7.1) Windows 98 □Version 4.10.2222□ tally13 hdl8 2 test-hdl SWB-33 Rumpole JRL r 6F 2B 1F Shutdown Test PC

Log File Highlights:	***** Monitor Execution *****
	Monitor BIOS interrupt 13h (disk service)
	tally13 compiled on 07/29/03 at 07:33:17
	@(#) Version 1.1 Created 07/29/03 at 07:28:05
	Now (08/31/03 at 08:26:23) Going . . . TSR
	***** Install HDL Log *****
	HDL -- Int_13 Hard Disk Write Lock V0.8 021126 (c)RCMP 1993-2002
	      ---- Royal Canadian Mounted Police ----
	      UNAUTHORIZED USE / DISTRIBUTION PROHIBITED
	
	      Licensee: US Dept. Commerce / NIST S/W Testing
	      3 Hard-Disks reported by Int_13h
	      Hard-Disk 0 Not Locked!
	      Hard-Disk 1 Not Locked!
	      Hard-Disk 2 Locked!
	      Write Lock successfully installed.
	***** Test Harness Log *****
	CMD: A:\TEST-HDL.EXE SWB-33 Rumpole JRL r 6F 2B 1F
	Case: SWB-33
	Command set: Read
	Date: Sun Aug 31 08:26:26 2003
	
	Version: @(#) test-hdl.cpp Version 1.1 Created 08/23/03 at 10:13:51
	      @(#) wb-defs.h Version 1.2 Created 08/31/03 at 08:18:19
	      Compiled on Aug 31 2003 at 08:10:54
	Operator: JRL
	Host: Rumpole
	Number of drives 3, Drives: 6F 2B 1F
	    Case Cmd Drv Action Stat Cry Count Cmd Name
	 0 SWB-33 <02> 80 Allowed 0000 Off 1 ReadSectors
	 1 SWB-33 <0A> 80 Allowed 0000 Off 1 ReadLong
	 2 SWB-33 <42> 80 Allowed 0000 Off 1 ExtRead
	Results for SWB-33 category r on drive 80 No commands blocked (0 of 3)
	 0 SWB-33 <02> 81 Allowed 0000 Off 1 ReadSectors
	 1 SWB-33 <0A> 81 Allowed 0000 Off 1 ReadLong
	 2 SWB-33 <42> 81 Allowed 0000 Off 1 ExtRead
	Results for SWB-33 category r on drive 81 No commands blocked (0 of 3)
	 0 SWB-33 <02> 82 Allowed 0000 Off 1 ReadSectors
	 1 SWB-33 <0A> 82 Allowed 0000 Off 1 ReadLong
	 2 SWB-33 <42> 82 Allowed 0000 Off 1 ExtRead
	Results for SWB-33 category r on drive 82 No commands blocked (0 of 3)
	Summary: 9 sent, 0 blocked, 9 not blocked

Results:	

Assertion	Expected Results	Actual Results
AM-07	Tool active message	Tool active message
AM-08	3 drives identified	3 drives identified
AM-09	Drive 80 is unprotected	Drive 80 is unprotected
AM-09	Drive 81 is unprotected	Drive 81 is unprotected

Case SWB-33 HDL -- Int_13 Hard Disk Write Lock V0.8 021126 © RCMP 1993-2002			
	AM-09	Drive 82 is protected	Drive 82 is protected
	AM-11	0 Commands return fail	0 Commands return fail
	AO-04	No cmds to drive 82 blocked	No cmds to drive 82 blocked
	AO-07	No cmds to drive 80 blocked	No cmds to drive 80 blocked
	AO-07	No cmds to drive 81 blocked	No cmds to drive 81 blocked
Analysis:	SWB-33 Expected results achieved		

Case SWB-34 HDL -- Int_13 Hard Disk Write Lock V0.8 021126 © RCMP 1993-2002	
Case Summary:	SWB-34 Install three drives, configure return code to success, protect with pattern UPP, execute read commands.
Assertions Tested:	SWB-AM-07. If the tool is executed then the tool shall issue a message indicating that the tool is active. SWB-AM-08. If the tool is executed then the tool shall issue a message indicating all drives accessible by the covered interfaces. SWB-AM-09. If the tool is executed then the tool shall issue a message indicating the protection status of each drive attached to a covered interface. SWB-AM-10. If the tool is configured to return success on blocked commands and the tool blocks a command then the return code shall indicate successful command execution. SWB-AO-04. If a subset of all covered drives is specified for protection, then commands from the read category shall not be blocked for drives in the selected subset. SWB-AO-07. If a subset of all covered drives is specified for protection, then no commands from any category shall be blocked for drives not in the selected subset.
Tester Name:	JRL
Test Date:	Sun Aug 31 09:26:05 2003
Test PC:	McCloud
Test Software:	SWBT 1.0
Hard Drives Used:	Drive 80, label 8A is a WDC WD200EB-00CSF0 with 39102336 sectors Drive 81, label F5 is an IBM-DTLA-307020 with 40188960 sectors Drive 82, label F6 is an IBM-DTLA-307020 with 40188960 sectors
Commands Executed:	Boot Test PC to (DOS 7.1) Windows 98 ☐Version 4.10.2222☐ tally13 hdl8 S12 test-hdl SWB-34 McCloud JRL r 8A F5 F6 Shutdown Test PC
Log File Highlights:	***** Monitor Execution ***** Monitor BIOS interrupt 13h (disk service) tally13 compiled on 07/29/03 at 07:33:17 @(#) Version 1.1 Created 07/29/03 at 07:28:05 Now (08/31/03 at 09:25:58) Going . . . TSR ***** Install HDL Log ***** HDL -- Int_13 Hard Disk Write Lock V0.8 021126 (c)RCMP 1993-2002 ---- Royal Canadian Mounted Police ---- UNAUTHORIZED USE / DISTRIBUTION PROHIBITED Licensee: US Dept. Commerce / NIST S/W Testing 3 Hard-Disks reported by Int_13h Hard-Disk 0 Not Locked! Hard-Disk 1 Locked! Hard-Disk 2 Locked! Write Lock successfully installed. ***** Test Harness Log ***** CMD: A:\TEST-HDL.EXE SWB-34 McCloud JRL r 8A F5 F6 Case: SWB-34 Command set: Read Date: Sun Aug 31 09:26:05 2003 Version: @(#) test-hdl.cpp Version 1.1 Created 08/23/03 at 10:13:51 @(#) wb-defs.h Version 1.2 Created 08/31/03 at 08:18:19 Compiled on Aug 31 2003 at 08:10:54 Operator: JRL Host: McCloud Number of drives 3, Drives: 8A F5 F6 Case Cmd Drv Action Stat Cry Count Cmd Name 0 SWB-34 <02> 80 Allowed 0000 Off 1 ReadSectors 1 SWB-34 <0A> 80 Allowed 0000 Off 1 ReadLong 2 SWB-34 <42> 80 Allowed 0000 Off 1 ExtRead

	Results for SWB-34 category r on drive 80 No commands blocked (0 of 3)
	  0 SWB-34 <02> 81 Allowed 0000 Off 1 ReadSectors
	  1 SWB-34 <0A> 81 Allowed 0000 Off 1 ReadLong
	  2 SWB-34 <42> 81 Allowed 0000 Off 1 ExtRead
	Results for SWB-34 category r on drive 81 No commands blocked (0 of 3)
	  0 SWB-34 <02> 82 Allowed 0000 Off 1 ReadSectors
	  1 SWB-34 <0A> 82 Allowed 0000 Off 1 ReadLong
	  2 SWB-34 <42> 82 Allowed 0000 Off 1 ExtRead
	Results for SWB-34 category r on drive 82 No commands blocked (0 of 3)
	Summary: 9 sent, 0 blocked, 9 not blocked

Results:	

Assertion	Expected Results	Actual Results
AM-07	Tool active message	Tool active message
AM-08	3 drives identified	3 drives identified
AM-09	Drive 80 is unprotected	Drive 80 is unprotected
AM-09	Drive 81 is protected	Drive 81 is protected
AM-09	Drive 82 is protected	Drive 82 is protected
AM-10	0 Commands return success	0 Commands return success
AO-04	No cmds to drive 81 blocked	No cmds to drive 81 blocked
AO-04	No cmds to drive 82 blocked	No cmds to drive 82 blocked
AO-07	No cmds to drive 80 blocked	No cmds to drive 80 blocked

Analysis:	SWB-34 Expected results achieved

Case Summary:	SWB-35 Install three drives, configure return code to failure, protect with pattern PUP, execute read commands.
Assertions Tested:	SWB-AM-07. If the tool is executed then the tool shall issue a message indicating that the tool is active. SWB-AM-08. If the tool is executed then the tool shall issue a message indicating all drives accessible by the covered interfaces. SWB-AM-09. If the tool is executed then the tool shall issue a message indicating the protection status of each drive attached to a covered interface. SWB-AM-11. If the tool is configured to return fail on blocked commands and the tool blocks a command then the return code shall indicate unsuccessful command execution. SWB-AO-04. If a subset of all covered drives is specified for protection, then commands from the read category shall not be blocked for drives in the selected subset. SWB-AO-07. If a subset of all covered drives is specified for protection, then no commands from any category shall be blocked for drives not in the selected subset.
Tester Name:	JRL
Test Date:	Sun Aug 31 08:28:38 2003
Test PC:	Rumpole
Test Software:	SWBT 1.0
Hard Drives Used:	Drive 80, label 6F is a Maxtor 6□060L0 with 120103200 sectors Drive 81, label 2B is a □uantum □M39100TD-SCA Drive with 17783249 sectors Drive 82, label 1F is a □uantum ATLAS10□3_18_SCA Drive with 35916548 sectors
Commands Executed:	Boot Test PC to (DOS 7.1) Windows 98 □Version 4.10.2222□ tally13 hdl8 02 test-hdl SWB-35 Rumpole JRL r 6F 2B 1F Shutdown Test PC

Log File Highlights:	***** Monitor Execution *****
	Monitor BIOS interrupt 13h (disk service)
	tally13 compiled on 07/29/03 at 07:33:17
	@(#) Version 1.1 Created 07/29/03 at 07:28:05
	Now (08/31/03 at 08:28:35) Going . . . TSR
	***** Install HDL Log *****
	HDL -- Int_13 Hard Disk Write Lock V0.8 021126 (c)RCMP 1993-2002
	     ---- Royal Canadian Mounted Police ----
	    UNAUTHORIZED USE / DISTRIBUTION PROHIBITED
	
	    Licensee: US Dept. Commerce / NIST S/W Testing
	    3 Hard-Disks reported by Int_13h

```
                    Hard-Disk 0     Locked!
                    Hard-Disk 1 Not Locked!
                    Hard-Disk 2     Locked!
                    Write Lock successfully installed.
        ***** Test Harness Log *****
        CMD: A:\TEST-HDL.EXE SWB-35 Rumpole JRL r 6F 2B 1F
        Case: SWB-35
        Command set: Read
        Date: Sun Aug 31 08:28:38 2003

        Version: @(#) test-hdl.cpp Version 1.1 Created 08/23/03 at 10:13:51
                @(#) wb-defs.h Version 1.2 Created 08/31/03 at 08:18:19
                Compiled on Aug 31 2003 at 08:10:54
        Operator: JRL
        Host: Rumpole
        Number of drives 3, Drives: 6F 2B 1F
            Case  Cmd Drv Action  Stat Cry Count Cmd Name
         0 SWB-35 <02> 80 Allowed 0000 Off    1  ReadSectors
         1 SWB-35 <0A> 80 Allowed 0000 Off    1  ReadLong
         2 SWB-35 <42> 80 Allowed 0000 Off    1  ExtRead
        Results for SWB-35 category r on drive 80 No commands blocked (0 of 3)
         0 SWB-35 <02> 81 Allowed 0000 Off    1  ReadSectors
         1 SWB-35 <0A> 81 Allowed 0000 Off    1  ReadLong
         2 SWB-35 <42> 81 Allowed 0000 Off    1  ExtRead
        Results for SWB-35 category r on drive 81 No commands blocked (0 of 3)
         0 SWB-35 <02> 82 Allowed 0000 Off    1  ReadSectors
         1 SWB-35 <0A> 82 Allowed 0000 Off    1  ReadLong
         2 SWB-35 <42> 82 Allowed 0000 Off    1  ExtRead
        Results for SWB-35 category r on drive 82 No commands blocked (0 of 3)
        Summary: 9 sent, 0 blocked, 9 not blocked
```

Results:			
	Assertion	**Expected Results**	**Actual Results**
	AM-07	Tool active message	Tool active message
	AM-08	3 drives identified	3 drives identified
	AM-09	Drive 80 is protected	Drive 80 is protected
	AM-09	Drive 81 is unprotected	Drive 81 is unprotected
	AM-09	Drive 82 is protected	Drive 82 is protected
	AM-11	0 Commands return fail	0 Commands return fail
	AO-04	No cmds to drive 80 blocked	No cmds to drive 80 blocked
	AO-04	No cmds to drive 82 blocked	No cmds to drive 82 blocked
	AO-07	No cmds to drive 81 blocked	No cmds to drive 81 blocked

Analysis:	SWB-35 Expected results achieved

Case Summary:	SWB-36 Install three drives, configure return code to success, protect with pattern PPU, execute read commands.
Assertions Tested:	SWB-AM-07. If the tool is executed then the tool shall issue a message indicating that the tool is active. SWB-AM-08. If the tool is executed then the tool shall issue a message indicating all drives accessible by the covered interfaces. SWB-AM-09. If the tool is executed then the tool shall issue a message indicating the protection status of each drive attached to a covered interface. SWB-AM-10. If the tool is configured to return success on blocked commands and the tool blocks a command then the return code shall indicate successful command execution. SWB-AO-04. If a subset of all covered drives is specified for protection, then commands from the read category shall not be blocked for drives in the selected subset. SWB-AO-07. If a subset of all covered drives is specified for protection, then no commands from any category shall be blocked for drives not in the selected subset.
Tester Name:	JRL
Test Date:	Sun Aug 31 09:18:20 2003
Test PC:	Wimsey
Test Software:	SWBT 1.0
Hard Drives Used:	Drive 80, label 90 is a WDC WD300BB-00CAA0 with 58633344 sectors Drive 81, label 64 is a WDC WD64AA with 12594960 sectors

	Case SWB-36 HDL -- Int_13 Hard Disk Write Lock V0.8 021126 © RCMP 1993-2002
	Drive 82, label E3 is a □UANTUM ATLAS10□2-T□092J with 17938985 sectors
Commands Executed:	Boot Test PC to (DOS 7.1) Windows 98 □Version 4.10.2222□ tally13 hdl8 S01 test-hdl SWB-36 Wimsey JRL r 90 64 E3 Shutdown Test PC

Log File Highlights:	***** Monitor Execution *****
	Monitor BIOS interrupt 13h (disk service)
	tally13 compiled on 07/29/03 at 07:33:17
	@(#) Version 1.1 Created 07/29/03 at 07:28:05
	Now (08/31/03 at 09:18:18) Going . . . TSR
	***** Install HDL Log *****
	HDL -- Int_13 Hard Disk Write Lock V0.8 021126 (c)RCMP 1993-2002
	    ---- Royal Canadian Mounted Police ----
	    UNAUTHORIZED USE / DISTRIBUTION PROHIBITED
	
	    Licensee: US Dept. Commerce / NIST S/W Testing
	    3 Hard-Disks reported by Int_13h
	    Hard-Disk 0 Locked!
	    Hard-Disk 1 Locked!
	    Hard-Disk 2 Not Locked!
	    Write Lock successfully installed.
	***** Test Harness Log *****
	CMD: A:\TEST-HDL.EXE SWB-36 Wimsey JRL r 90 64 E3
	Case: SWB-36
	Command set: Read
	Date: Sun Aug 31 09:18:20 2003
	
	Version: @(#) test-hdl.cpp Version 1.1 Created 08/23/03 at 10:13:51
	     @(#) wb-defs.h Version 1.2 Created 08/31/03 at 08:18:19
	     Compiled on Aug 31 2003 at 08:10:54
	Operator: JRL
	Host: Wimsey
	Number of drives 3, Drives: 90 64 E3
	    Case Cmd Drv Action Stat Cry Count Cmd Name
	 0 SWB-36 <02> 80 Allowed 0000 Off 1 ReadSectors
	 1 SWB-36 <0A> 80 Allowed 0000 Off 1 ReadLong
	 2 SWB-36 <42> 80 Allowed 0000 Off 1 ExtRead
	Results for SWB-36 category r on drive 80 No commands blocked (0 of 3)
	 0 SWB-36 <02> 81 Allowed 0000 Off 1 ReadSectors
	 1 SWB-36 <0A> 81 Allowed 0000 Off 1 ReadLong
	 2 SWB-36 <42> 81 Allowed 0000 Off 1 ExtRead
	Results for SWB-36 category r on drive 81 No commands blocked (0 of 3)
	 0 SWB-36 <02> 82 Allowed 0000 Off 1 ReadSectors
	 1 SWB-36 <0A> 82 Allowed 0000 Off 1 ReadLong
	 2 SWB-36 <42> 82 Allowed 0000 Off 1 ExtRead
	Results for SWB-36 category r on drive 82 No commands blocked (0 of 3)
	Summary: 9 sent, 0 blocked, 9 not blocked

Results:

Assertion	Expected Results	Actual Results
AM-07	Tool active message	Tool active message
AM-08	3 drives identified	3 drives identified
AM-09	Drive 80 is protected	Drive 80 is protected
AM-09	Drive 81 is protected	Drive 81 is protected
AM-09	Drive 82 is unprotected	Drive 82 is unprotected
AM-10	0 Commands return success	0 Commands return success
AO-04	No cmds to drive 80 blocked	No cmds to drive 80 blocked
AO-04	No cmds to drive 81 blocked	No cmds to drive 81 blocked
AO-07	No cmds to drive 82 blocked	No cmds to drive 82 blocked

Analysis:	SWB-36 Expected results achieved

	Case SWB-37 HDL -- Int_13 Hard Disk Write Lock V0.8 021126 © RCMP 1993-2002
Case Summary:	SWB-37 Install all drives, configure to be active at boot and shutdown, configure return code to failure, protect with pattern odd, execute write commands.
Assertions Tested:	SWB-AM-07. If the tool is executed then the tool shall issue a message indicating that the tool is active. SWB-AM-08. If the tool is executed then the tool shall issue a message

	indicating all drives accessible by the covered interfaces. SWB-AM-09. If the tool is executed then the tool shall issue a message indicating the protection status of each drive attached to a covered interface. SWB-AM-11. If the tool is configured to return fail on blocked commands and the tool blocks a command then the return code shall indicate unsuccessful command execution. SWB-AO-08. If the tool is active during the operating system boot and shutdown processes then no changes are made to any protected drives.
Tester Name:	JRL
Test Date:	Sun Aug 31 09:59:58 2003
Test PC:	Wimsey
Test Software:	SWBT 1.0
Hard Drives Used:	Drive 80, label 90 is a WDC WD300BB-00CAA0 with 58633344 sectors Drive 81, label 8A is a WDC WD200EB-00CSF0 with 39102336 sectors Drive 82, label E4 is a □UANTUM ATLAS10□2-T□092J with 17938985 sectors Drive 83, label 2B is a □uantum □M39100TD-SCA Drive with 17783249 sectors
Commands Executed:	Boot Host (HDL in AUTOEXEC.BAT) Windows 98 □Version 4.10.2222□ tally13 hdl8 13 test-hdl SWB-37 Wimsey JRL w 90 8A E4 2B Shutdown Host

Log File Highlights:	***** Monitor Execution *****
	Monitor BIOS interrupt 13h (disk service)
	tally13 compiled on 07/29/03 at 07:33:17
	@(#) Version 1.1 Created 07/29/03 at 07:28:05
	Now (08/31/03 at 09:56:55) Going . . . TSR
	***** Install HDL Log *****
	HDL -- Int_13 Hard Disk Write Lock V0.8 021126 (c)RCMP 1993-2002
	    ---- Royal Canadian Mounted Police ----
	      UNAUTHORIZED USE / DISTRIBUTION PROHIBITED
	
	    Licensee: US Dept. Commerce / NIST S/W Testing
	    4 Hard-Disks reported by Int_13h
	    Hard-Disk 0 Not Locked!
	    Hard-Disk 1 Locked!
	    Hard-Disk 2 Not Locked!
	    Hard-Disk 3 Locked!
	    Write Lock successfully installed.
	***** Test Harness Log *****
	CMD: A:\TEST-HDL.EXE SWB-37 Wimsey JRL w 90 8A E4 2B
	Case: SWB-37
	Command set: Write
	Date: Sun Aug 31 09:59:58 2003
	
	Version: @(#) test-hdl.cpp Version 1.1 Created 08/23/03 at 10:13:51
	     @(#) wb-defs.h Version 1.2 Created 08/31/03 at 08:18:19
	     Compiled on Aug 31 2003 at 08:10:54
	Operator: JRL
	Host: Wimsey
	Number of drives 4, Drives: 90 8A E4 2B
	    Case Cmd Drv Action Stat Cry Count Cmd Name
	  0 SWB-37 <03> 80 Allowed 0000 Off 1 WriteSectors
	  1 SWB-37 <0B> 80 Allowed 0000 Off 1 WriteLong
	  2 SWB-37 <43> 80 Allowed 0000 Off 1 ExtWrite
	Results for SWB-37 category w on drive 80 No commands blocked (0 of 3)
	  0 SWB-37 <03> 81 Blocked 0300 On 0 WriteSectors
	  1 SWB-37 <0B> 81 Blocked 0300 On 0 WriteLong
	  2 SWB-37 <43> 81 Blocked 0300 On 0 ExtWrite
	Results for SWB-37 category w on drive 81 All commands blocked (3 of 3)
	  0 SWB-37 <03> 82 Allowed 0000 Off 1 WriteSectors
	  1 SWB-37 <0B> 82 Allowed 0000 Off 1 WriteLong
	  2 SWB-37 <43> 82 Allowed 0000 Off 1 ExtWrite
	Results for SWB-37 category w on drive 82 No commands blocked (0 of 3)
	  0 SWB-37 <03> 83 Blocked 0300 On 0 WriteSectors
	  1 SWB-37 <0B> 83 Blocked 0300 On 0 WriteLong
	  2 SWB-37 <43> 83 Blocked 0300 On 0 ExtWrite
	Results for SWB-37 category w on drive 83 All commands blocked (3 of 3)
	Summary: 12 sent, 6 blocked, 6 not blocked

Results:			

Assertion	Expected Results	Actual Results
AM-07	Tool active message	Tool active message
AM-08	4 drives identified	4 drives identified
AM-09	Drive 80 is unprotected	Drive 80 is unprotected
AM-09	Drive 81 is protected	Drive 81 is protected
AM-09	Drive 82 is unprotected	Drive 82 is unprotected
AM-09	Drive 83 is protected	Drive 83 is protected
AM-11	6 Commands return fail	6 Commands return fail
AO-08	All cmds to drive 81 blocked	All cmds to drive 81 blocked
AO-08	All cmds to drive 83 blocked	All cmds to drive 83 blocked
AO-08	No cmds to drive 80 blocked	No cmds to drive 80 blocked
AO-08	No cmds to drive 82 blocked	No cmds to drive 82 blocked

Analysis:	SWB-37 Expected results achieved

Case Summary:	SWB-38 Install all drives, configure to be active at boot and shutdown, configure return code to success, protect with pattern even, execute write commands.
Assertions Tested:	SWB-AM-07. If the tool is executed then the tool shall issue a message indicating that the tool is active. SWB-AM-08. If the tool is executed then the tool shall issue a message indicating all drives accessible by the covered interfaces. SWB-AM-09. If the tool is executed then the tool shall issue a message indicating the protection status of each drive attached to a covered interface. SWB-AM-10. If the tool is configured to return success on blocked commands and the tool blocks a command then the return code shall indicate successful command execution. SWB-AO-08. If the tool is active during the operating system boot and shutdown processes then no changes are made to any protected drives.
Tester Name:	JRL
Test Date:	Sun Aug 31 09:22:47 2003
Test PC:	McMillan
Test Software:	SWBT 1.0
Hard Drives Used:	Drive 80, label F6 is an IBM-DTLA-307020 with 40188960 sectors Drive 81, label 6F is a Maxtor 6□060L0 with 120103200 sectors Drive 82, label 64 is a WDC WD64AA with 12594960 sectors Drive 83, label E3 is a □UANTUM ATLAS10□2-T□092J with 17938985 sectors Drive 84, label 1F is a □uantum ATLAS10□3_18_SCA Drive with 35916548 sectors
Commands Executed:	Boot Host (HDL in AUTOEXEC.BAT) Windows 98 □Version 4.10.2222□ tally13 hdl8 S024 test-hdl SWB-38 McMillan JRL w F6 6F 64 E3 1F Shutdown Host

Log File Highlights:	***** Monitor Execution *****
	Monitor BIOS interrupt 13h (disk service)
	tally13 compiled on 07/29/03 at 07:33:17
	@(#) Version 1.1 Created 07/29/03 at 07:28:05
	Now (08/31/03 at 09:20:25) Going . . . TSR
	***** Install HDL Log *****
	HDL -- Int_13 Hard Disk Write Lock V0.8 021126 (c)RCMP 1993-2002
	    ---- Royal Canadian Mounted Police ----
	    UNAUTHORIZED USE / DISTRIBUTION PROHIBITED
	
	    Licensee: US Dept. Commerce / NIST S/W Testing
	    5 Hard-Disks reported by Int_13h
	    Hard-Disk 0 Locked!
	    Hard-Disk 1 Not Locked!
	    Hard-Disk 2 Locked!
	    Hard-Disk 3 Not Locked!
	    Hard-Disk 4 Locked!

```
                    Write Lock successfully installed.
***** Test Harness Log *****
CMD: A:\TEST-HDL.EXE SWB-38 McMillan JRL w F6 6F 64 E3 1F
Case: SWB-38
Command set: Write
Date: Sun Aug 31 09:22:47 2003

Version: @(#) test-hdl.cpp Version 1.1 Created 08/23/03 at 10:13:51
         @(#) wb-defs.h Version 1.2 Created 08/31/03 at 08:18:19
         Compiled on Aug 31 2003 at 08:10:54
Operator: JRL
Host: McMillan
Number of drives 5, Drives: F6 6F 64 E3 1F
      Case  Cmd Drv Action  Stat Cry Count Cmd Name
  0 SWB-38 <03> 80 Blocked 0000 Off     0  WriteSectors
  1 SWB-38 <0B> 80 Blocked 0000 Off     0  WriteLong
  2 SWB-38 <43> 80 Blocked 0000 Off     0  ExtWrite
Results for SWB-38 category w on drive 80 All commands blocked (3 of 3)
  0 SWB-38 <03> 81 Allowed 0000 Off     1  WriteSectors
  1 SWB-38 <0B> 81 Allowed 0000 Off     1  WriteLong
  2 SWB-38 <43> 81 Allowed 0000 Off     1  ExtWrite
Results for SWB-38 category w on drive 81 No commands blocked (0 of 3)
  0 SWB-38 <03> 82 Blocked 0000 Off     0  WriteSectors
  1 SWB-38 <0B> 82 Blocked 0000 Off     0  WriteLong
  2 SWB-38 <43> 82 Blocked 0000 Off     0  ExtWrite
Results for SWB-38 category w on drive 82 All commands blocked (3 of 3)
  0 SWB-38 <03> 83 Allowed 0000 Off     1  WriteSectors
  1 SWB-38 <0B> 83 Allowed 0000 Off     1  WriteLong
  2 SWB-38 <43> 83 Allowed 0000 Off     1  ExtWrite
Results for SWB-38 category w on drive 83 No commands blocked (0 of 3)
  0 SWB-38 <03> 84 Blocked 0000 Off     0  WriteSectors
  1 SWB-38 <0B> 84 Blocked 0000 Off     0  WriteLong
  2 SWB-38 <43> 84 Blocked 0000 Off     0  ExtWrite
Results for SWB-38 category w on drive 84 All commands blocked (3 of 3)
Summary: 15 sent, 9 blocked, 6 not blocked
```

Results:

Assertion	Expected Results	Actual Results
AM-07	Tool active message	Tool active message
AM-08	5 drives identified	5 drives identified
AM-09	Drive 80 is protected	Drive 80 is protected
AM-09	Drive 81 is unprotected	Drive 81 is unprotected
AM-09	Drive 82 is protected	Drive 82 is protected
AM-09	Drive 83 is unprotected	Drive 83 is unprotected
AM-09	Drive 84 is protected	Drive 84 is protected
AM-10	9 Commands return success	9 Commands return success
AO-08	All cmds to drive 80 blocked	All cmds to drive 80 blocked
AO-08	All cmds to drive 82 blocked	All cmds to drive 82 blocked
AO-08	All cmds to drive 84 blocked	All cmds to drive 84 blocked
AO-08	No cmds to drive 81 blocked	No cmds to drive 81 blocked
AO-08	No cmds to drive 83 blocked	No cmds to drive 83 blocked

Analysis: SWB-38 Expected results achieved

Case Summary:	SWB-39 Install all drives, configure return code to failure, protect with pattern high, execute write commands, uninstall, execute all commands.
Assertions Tested:	SWB-AM-07. If the tool is executed then the tool shall issue a message indicating that the tool is active. SWB-AM-08. If the tool is executed then the tool shall issue a message indicating all drives accessible by the covered interfaces. SWB-AM-09. If the tool is executed then the tool shall issue a message indicating the protection status of each drive attached to a covered interface. SWB-AM-11. If the tool is configured to return fail on blocked commands and the tool blocks a command then the return code shall indicate

	unsuccessful command execution. SWB-AO-09. If the tool is active and the tool is then uninstalled then no commands to any drive shall be blocked.
Tester Name:	JRL
Test Date:	Tue Sep 02 08:15:21 2003
Test PC:	Cadfael
Test Software:	SWBT 1.0
Hard Drives Used:	Drive 80, label F5 is an IBM-DTLA-307020 with 40188960 sectors Drive 81, label 64 is a WDC WD64AA with 12594960 sectors Drive 82, label E3 is a □UANTUM ATLAS10□2-T□092J with 17938985 sectors Drive 83, label 2B is a □uantum □M39100TD-SCA Drive with 17783249 sectors
Commands Executed:	Boot Test PC Windows 98 □Version 4.10.2222□ tally13 hdl8 23 test-hdl SWB-39 Cadfael JRL w F5 64 E3 2B t-off SWB-39 Cadfael JRL hdl8 R test-hdl SWB-39 Cadfael JRL a F5 64 E3 2B Shutdown Test PC

Log File
Highlights:
	***** Monitor Execution *****
	Monitor BIOS interrupt 13h (disk service)
	tally13 compiled on 07/29/03 at 07:33:17
	@(#) Version 1.1 Created 07/29/03 at 07:28:05
	Now (09/02/03 at 08:15:00) Going . . . TSR
	***** Install HDL Log *****
	HDL -- Int_13 Hard Disk Write Lock V0.8 021126 (c)RCMP 1993-2002
	    ---- Royal Canadian Mounted Police ----
	    UNAUTHORIZED USE / DISTRIBUTION PROHIBITED
	
	    Licensee: US Dept. Commerce / NIST S/W Testing
	    4 Hard-Disks reported by Int_13h
	    Hard-Disk 0 Not Locked!
	    Hard-Disk 1 Not Locked!
	    Hard-Disk 2 Locked!
	    Hard-Disk 3 Locked!
	    Write Lock successfully installed.
	***** Blocked Write Commands *****
	CMD: a:\TEST-HDL.EXE SWB-39 Cadfael JRL w F5 64 E3 2B
	Case: SWB-39
	Command set: Write
	Date: Tue Sep 02 08:15:07 2003
	
	Version: @(#) test-hdl.cpp Version 1.1 Created 08/23/03 at 10:13:51
	    @(#) wb-defs.h Version 1.2 Created 08/31/03 at 08:18:19
	    Compiled on Aug 31 2003 at 08:10:54
	Operator: JRL
	Host: Cadfael
	Number of drives 4, Drives: F5 64 E3 2B
	    Case Cmd Drv Action Stat Cry Count Cmd Name
	  0 SWB-39 <03> 80 Allowed 0000 Off 1 WriteSectors
	  1 SWB-39 <0B> 80 Allowed 0000 Off 1 WriteLong
	  2 SWB-39 <43> 80 Allowed 0000 Off 1 ExtWrite
	Results for SWB-39 category w on drive 80 No commands blocked (0 of 3)
	  0 SWB-39 <03> 81 Allowed 0000 Off 1 WriteSectors
	  1 SWB-39 <0B> 81 Allowed 0000 Off 1 WriteLong
	  2 SWB-39 <43> 81 Allowed 0000 Off 1 ExtWrite
	Results for SWB-39 category w on drive 81 No commands blocked (0 of 3)
	  0 SWB-39 <03> 82 Blocked 0300 On 0 WriteSectors
	  1 SWB-39 <0B> 82 Blocked 0300 On 0 WriteLong
	  2 SWB-39 <43> 82 Blocked 0300 On 0 ExtWrite
	Results for SWB-39 category w on drive 82 All commands blocked (3 of 3)
	  0 SWB-39 <03> 83 Blocked 0300 On 0 WriteSectors
	  1 SWB-39 <0B> 83 Blocked 0300 On 0 WriteLong
	  2 SWB-39 <43> 83 Blocked 0300 On 0 ExtWrite
	Results for SWB-39 category w on drive 83 All commands blocked (3 of 3)
	Summary: 12 sent, 6 blocked, 6 not blocked
	
	Number of Commands not blocked (should total to 6)
	Drive Count

```
                     80        3
                     81        3
                     82        0
                     83        0
***** Uninstall HDL Log *****
HDL -- Int_13 Hard Disk Write Lock V0.8 021126 (c)RCMP 1993-2002
          ---- Royal Canadian Mounted Police ----
          UNAUTHORIZED USE / DISTRIBUTION PROHIBITED


          Licensee: US Dept. Commerce / NIST S/W Testing
          4  Hard-Disks reported by Int_13h
          Write Lock removed.
***** Test Harness Log *****
CMD: a:\TEST-HDL.EXE SWB-39 Cadfael JRL a F5 64 E3 2B
Case: SWB-39
Command set: All
Date: Tue Sep 02 08:15:21 2003


Version: @(#) test-hdl.cpp Version 1.1 Created 08/23/03 at 10:13:51
         @(#) wb-defs.h Version 1.2 Created 08/31/03 at 08:18:19
         Compiled on Aug 31 2003 at 08:10:54
Operator: JRL
Host: Cadfael
Number of drives 4, Drives: F5 64 E3 2B
Warning: non-□ero tally (3) for drive 80 (reboot to clear)
Warning: non-□ero tally (3) for drive 81 (reboot to clear)
       Case  Cmd Drv Action  Stat Cry Count Cmd Name
  0 SWB-39 <00> 80 Allowed 0000 Off     1  Reset
  1 SWB-39 <0C> 80 Allowed 0000 Off     1  SeekDrive
  2 SWB-39 <0D> 80 Allowed 0000 Off     1  AltReset
  3 SWB-39 <11> 80 Allowed 0000 Off     1  Recalibrate
  4 SWB-39 <47> 80 Allowed 0000 Off     1  ExtendedSeek
Results for SWB-39 category c on drive 80 No commands blocked (0 of 5)
  0 SWB-39 <00> 81 Allowed 0000 Off     1  Reset
  1 SWB-39 <0C> 81 Allowed 0000 Off     1  SeekDrive
  2 SWB-39 <0D> 81 Allowed 0000 Off     1  AltReset
  3 SWB-39 <11> 81 Allowed 0000 Off     1  Recalibrate
  4 SWB-39 <47> 81 Allowed 0000 Off     1  ExtendedSeek
Results for SWB-39 category c on drive 81 No commands blocked (0 of 5)
  0 SWB-39 <00> 82 Allowed 0000 Off     1  Reset
  1 SWB-39 <0C> 82 Allowed 0000 Off     1  SeekDrive
  2 SWB-39 <0D> 82 Allowed 0000 Off     1  AltReset
  3 SWB-39 <11> 82 Allowed 0000 Off     1  Recalibrate
  4 SWB-39 <47> 82 Allowed 0000 Off     1  ExtendedSeek
Results for SWB-39 category c on drive 82 No commands blocked (0 of 5)
  0 SWB-39 <00> 83 Allowed 0000 Off     1  Reset
  1 SWB-39 <0C> 83 Allowed 0000 Off     1  SeekDrive
  2 SWB-39 <0D> 83 Allowed 0000 Off     1  AltReset
  3 SWB-39 <11> 83 Allowed 0000 Off     1  Recalibrate
  4 SWB-39 <47> 83 Allowed 0000 Off     1  ExtendedSeek
Results for SWB-39 category c on drive 83 No commands blocked (0 of 5)
Summary: 20 sent, 0 blocked, 20 not blocked

  0 SWB-39 <01> 80 Allowed 0000 Off       1  GetLastStatus
  1 SWB-39 <04> 80 Allowed 0000 Off       1  VerifySectors
  2 SWB-39 <08> 80 Allowed 0000 Off       1  ReadDriveParms
  3 SWB-39 <10> 80 Allowed 0000 Off       1  TestDriveReady
  4 SWB-39 <15> 80 Allowed 0000 Off       1  ReadDriveType
  5 SWB-39 <41> 80 Allowed 0000 Off       1  CheckForExtensions
  6 SWB-39 <44> 80 Allowed 0000 Off       1  VerifySectors
  7 SWB-39 <48> 80 Allowed 0000 Off       1  GetDriveParms
Results for SWB-39 category i on drive 80 No commands blocked (0 of 8)
  0 SWB-39 <01> 81 Allowed 0000 Off       1  GetLastStatus
  1 SWB-39 <04> 81 Allowed 0000 Off       1  VerifySectors
  2 SWB-39 <08> 81 Allowed 0000 Off       1  ReadDriveParms
  3 SWB-39 <10> 81 Allowed 0000 Off       1  TestDriveReady
  4 SWB-39 <15> 81 Allowed 0000 Off       1  ReadDriveType
  5 SWB-39 <41> 81 Allowed 0000 Off       1  CheckForExtensions
  6 SWB-39 <44> 81 Allowed 0000 Off       1  VerifySectors
  7 SWB-39 <48> 81 Allowed 0000 Off       1  GetDriveParms
Results for SWB-39 category i on drive 81 No commands blocked (0 of 8)
  0 SWB-39 <01> 82 Allowed 0000 Off       1  GetLastStatus
  1 SWB-39 <04> 82 Allowed 0000 Off       1  VerifySectors
```

```
        2 SWB-39 <08> 82 Allowed 0000 Off      1   ReadDriveParms
        3 SWB-39 <10> 82 Allowed 0000 Off      1   TestDriveReady
        4 SWB-39 <15> 82 Allowed 0000 Off      1   ReadDriveType
        5 SWB-39 <41> 82 Allowed 0000 Off      1   CheckForExtensions
        6 SWB-39 <44> 82 Allowed 0000 Off      1   VerifySectors
        7 SWB-39 <48> 82 Allowed 0000 Off      1   GetDriveParms
Results for SWB-39 category i on drive 82 No commands blocked (0 of 8)
        0 SWB-39 <01> 83 Allowed 0000 Off      1   GetLastStatus
        1 SWB-39 <04> 83 Allowed 0000 Off      1   VerifySectors
        2 SWB-39 <08> 83 Allowed 0000 Off      1   ReadDriveParms
        3 SWB-39 <10> 83 Allowed 0000 Off      1   TestDriveReady
        4 SWB-39 <15> 83 Allowed 0000 Off      1   ReadDriveType
        5 SWB-39 <41> 83 Allowed 0000 Off      1   CheckForExtensions
        6 SWB-39 <44> 83 Allowed 0000 Off      1   VerifySectors
        7 SWB-39 <48> 83 Allowed 0000 Off      1   GetDriveParms
Results for SWB-39 category i on drive 83 No commands blocked (0 of 8)
Summary: 32 sent, 0 blocked, 32 not blocked

        0 SWB-39 <02> 80 Allowed 0000 Off      1   ReadSectors
        1 SWB-39 <0A> 80 Allowed 0000 Off      1   ReadLong
        2 SWB-39 <42> 80 Allowed 0000 Off      1   ExtRead
Results for SWB-39 category r on drive 80 No commands blocked (0 of 3)
        0 SWB-39 <02> 81 Allowed 0000 Off      1   ReadSectors
        1 SWB-39 <0A> 81 Allowed 0000 Off      1   ReadLong
        2 SWB-39 <42> 81 Allowed 0000 Off      1   ExtRead
Results for SWB-39 category r on drive 81 No commands blocked (0 of 3)
        0 SWB-39 <02> 82 Allowed 0000 Off      1   ReadSectors
        1 SWB-39 <0A> 82 Allowed 0000 Off      1   ReadLong
        2 SWB-39 <42> 82 Allowed 0000 Off      1   ExtRead
Results for SWB-39 category r on drive 82 No commands blocked (0 of 3)
        0 SWB-39 <02> 83 Allowed 0000 Off      1   ReadSectors
        1 SWB-39 <0A> 83 Allowed 0000 Off      1   ReadLong
        2 SWB-39 <42> 83 Allowed 0000 Off      1   ExtRead
Results for SWB-39 category r on drive 83 No commands blocked (0 of 3)
Summary: 12 sent, 0 blocked, 12 not blocked

        0 SWB-39 <03> 80 Allowed 0000 Off      2   WriteSectors
        1 SWB-39 <0B> 80 Allowed 0000 Off      2   WriteLong
        2 SWB-39 <43> 80 Allowed 0000 Off      2   ExtWrite
Results for SWB-39 category w on drive 80 No commands blocked (0 of 3)
        0 SWB-39 <03> 81 Allowed 0000 Off      2   WriteSectors
        1 SWB-39 <0B> 81 Allowed 0000 Off      2   WriteLong
        2 SWB-39 <43> 81 Allowed 0000 Off      2   ExtWrite
Results for SWB-39 category w on drive 81 No commands blocked (0 of 3)
        0 SWB-39 <03> 82 Allowed 0000 Off      1   WriteSectors
        1 SWB-39 <0B> 82 Allowed 0000 Off      1   WriteLong
        2 SWB-39 <43> 82 Allowed 0000 Off      1   ExtWrite
Results for SWB-39 category w on drive 82 No commands blocked (0 of 3)
        0 SWB-39 <03> 83 Allowed 0000 Off      1   WriteSectors
        1 SWB-39 <0B> 83 Allowed 0000 Off      1   WriteLong
        2 SWB-39 <43> 83 Allowed 0000 Off      1   ExtWrite
Results for SWB-39 category w on drive 83 No commands blocked (0 of 3)
Summary: 12 sent, 0 blocked, 12 not blocked

        0 SWB-39 <05> 80 Allowed 0000 Off      1   FormatTrack
        1 SWB-39 <06> 80 Allowed 0000 Off      1   FormatBadSectors
        2 SWB-39 <07> 80 Allowed 0000 Off      1   FormatCyl
        3 SWB-39 <09> 80 Allowed 0000 Off      1   InitDriveParms
        4 SWB-39 <0E> 80 Allowed 0000 Off      1   DiagnosticESDI
        5 SWB-39 <0F> 80 Allowed 0000 Off      1   DiagnosticESDI
        6 SWB-39 <12> 80 Allowed 0000 Off      1   DiagnosticRAM
        7 SWB-39 <13> 80 Allowed 0000 Off      1   DiagnosticDrive
        8 SWB-39 <14> 80 Allowed 0000 Off      1   DiagnosticCTL
Results for SWB-39 category x on drive 80 No commands blocked (0 of 9)
        0 SWB-39 <05> 81 Allowed 0000 Off      1   FormatTrack
        1 SWB-39 <06> 81 Allowed 0000 Off      1   FormatBadSectors
        2 SWB-39 <07> 81 Allowed 0000 Off      1   FormatCyl
        3 SWB-39 <09> 81 Allowed 0000 Off      1   InitDriveParms
        4 SWB-39 <0E> 81 Allowed 0000 Off      1   DiagnosticESDI
        5 SWB-39 <0F> 81 Allowed 0000 Off      1   DiagnosticESDI
        6 SWB-39 <12> 81 Allowed 0000 Off      1   DiagnosticRAM
        7 SWB-39 <13> 81 Allowed 0000 Off      1   DiagnosticDrive
        8 SWB-39 <14> 81 Allowed 0000 Off      1   DiagnosticCTL
```

```
Results for SWB-39 category x on drive 81 No commands blocked (0 of 9)
    0 SWB-39 <05> 82 Allowed 0000 Off      1  FormatTrack
    1 SWB-39 <06> 82 Allowed 0000 Off      1  FormatBadSectors
    2 SWB-39 <07> 82 Allowed 0000 Off      1  FormatCyl
    3 SWB-39 <09> 82 Allowed 0000 Off      1  InitDriveParms
    4 SWB-39 <0E> 82 Allowed 0000 Off      1  DiagnosticESDI
    5 SWB-39 <0F> 82 Allowed 0000 Off      1  DiagnosticESDI
    6 SWB-39 <12> 82 Allowed 0000 Off      1  DiagnosticRAM
    7 SWB-39 <13> 82 Allowed 0000 Off      1  DiagnosticDrive
    8 SWB-39 <14> 82 Allowed 0000 Off      1  DiagnosticCTL
Results for SWB-39 category x on drive 82 No commands blocked (0 of 9)
    0 SWB-39 <05> 83 Allowed 0000 Off      1  FormatTrack
    1 SWB-39 <06> 83 Allowed 0000 Off      1  FormatBadSectors
    2 SWB-39 <07> 83 Allowed 0000 Off      1  FormatCyl
    3 SWB-39 <09> 83 Allowed 0000 Off      1  InitDriveParms
    4 SWB-39 <0E> 83 Allowed 0000 Off      1  DiagnosticESDI
    5 SWB-39 <0F> 83 Allowed 0000 Off      1  DiagnosticESDI
    6 SWB-39 <12> 83 Allowed 0000 Off      1  DiagnosticRAM
    7 SWB-39 <13> 83 Allowed 0000 Off      1  DiagnosticDrive
    8 SWB-39 <14> 83 Allowed 0000 Off      1  DiagnosticCTL
Results for SWB-39 category x on drive 83 No commands blocked (0 of 9)
Summary: 36 sent, 0 blocked, 36 not blocked

    0 SWB-39 <16> 80 Allowed 0000 Off      1 Undefined
            ...

            misc commands 17-FD results omitted

            see log files for full results


            ...


  226 SWB-39 <FE> 80 Allowed 0000 Off      1 Undefined
  227 SWB-39 <FF> 80 Allowed 0000 Off      1 Undefined
Results for SWB-39 category m on drive 80 No commands blocked (0 of
228)
    0 SWB-39 <16> 81 Allowed 0000 Off      1 Undefined
            ...

            misc commands 17-FD results omitted

            see log files for full results


            ...


  226 SWB-39 <FE> 81 Allowed 0000 Off      1 Undefined
  227 SWB-39 <FF> 81 Allowed 0000 Off      1 Undefined
Results for SWB-39 category m on drive 81 No commands blocked (0 of
228)
    0 SWB-39 <16> 82 Allowed 0000 Off      1 Undefined
            ...

            misc commands 17-FD results omitted

            see log files for full results


            ...


  226 SWB-39 <FE> 82 Allowed 0000 Off      1 Undefined
  227 SWB-39 <FF> 82 Allowed 0000 Off      1 Undefined
Results for SWB-39 category m on drive 82 No commands blocked (0 of
228)
    0 SWB-39 <16> 83 Allowed 0000 Off      1 Undefined
            ...

            misc commands 17-FD results omitted

            see log files for full results


            ...


  226 SWB-39 <FE> 83 Allowed 0000 Off      1 Undefined
  227 SWB-39 <FF> 83 Allowed 0000 Off      1 Undefined
```

Case SWB-39 HDL -- Int_13 Hard Disk Write Lock V0.8 021126 © RCMP 1993-2002

	Results for SWB-39 category m on drive 83 No commands blocked (0 of 228) Summary: 912 sent, 0 blocked, 912 not blocked
Results:	

Assertion	Expected Results	Actual Results
AM-07	Tool active message	Tool active message
AM-08	4 drives identified	4 drives identified
AM-09	Drive 80 is unprotected	Drive 80 is unprotected
AM-09	Drive 81 is unprotected	Drive 81 is unprotected
AM-09	Drive 82 is protected	Drive 82 is protected
AM-09	Drive 83 is protected	Drive 83 is protected
AM-11	0 Commands return fail	0 Commands return fail
AO-09	SWB removed	Write Lock removed.

Analysis:	SWB-39 Expected results achieved

Case SWB-40 HDL -- Int_13 Hard Disk Write Lock V0.8 021126 © RCMP 1993-2002

Case Summary:	SWB-40 Install all drives, configure return code to success, protect with pattern low, execute write commands, uninstall, execute all commands.
Assertions Tested:	SWB-AM-07. If the tool is executed then the tool shall issue a message indicating that the tool is active. SWB-AM-08. If the tool is executed then the tool shall issue a message indicating all drives accessible by the covered interfaces. SWB-AM-09. If the tool is executed then the tool shall issue a message indicating the protection status of each drive attached to a covered interface. SWB-AM-10. If the tool is configured to return success on blocked commands and the tool blocks a command then the return code shall indicate successful command execution. SWB-AO-09. If the tool is active and the tool is then uninstalled then no commands to any drive shall be blocked.
Tester Name:	JRL
Test Date:	Sun Aug 31 09:27:36 2003
Test PC:	McMillan
Test Software:	SWBT 1.0
Hard Drives Used:	Drive 80, label F6 is an IBM-DTLA-307020 with 40188960 sectors Drive 81, label 6F is a Maxtor 6☐060L0 with 120103200 sectors Drive 82, label 64 is a WDC WD64AA with 12594960 sectors Drive 83, label E3 is a ☐UANTUM ATLAS10☐2-T☐092J with 17938985 sectors Drive 84, label 1F is a ☐uantum ATLAS10☐3_18_SCA Drive with 35916548 sectors
Commands Executed:	Boot Test PC Windows 98 ☐Version 4.10.2222☐ tally13 hdl8 S01 test-hdl SWB-40 McMillan JRL w F6 6F 64 E3 1F t-off SWB-40 McMillan JRL hdl8 R test-hdl SWB-40 McMillan JRL a F6 6F 64 E3 1F Shutdown Test PC

Log File Highlights:	***** Monitor Execution *****
	Monitor BIOS interrupt 13h (disk service)
	tally13 compiled on 07/29/03 at 07:33:17
	@(#) Version 1.1 Created 07/29/03 at 07:28:05
	Now (08/31/03 at 09:27:13) Going . . . TSR
	***** Install HDL Log *****
	HDL -- Int_13 Hard Disk Write Lock V0.8 021126 (c)RCMP 1993-2002
	    ---- Royal Canadian Mounted Police ----
	    UNAUTHORIZED USE / DISTRIBUTION PROHIBITED
	
	    Licensee: US Dept. Commerce / NIST S/W Testing
	    5 Hard-Disks reported by Int_13h
	    Hard-Disk 0 Locked!
	    Hard-Disk 1 Locked!
	    Hard-Disk 2 Not Locked!
	    Hard-Disk 3 Not Locked!
	    Hard-Disk 4 Not Locked!

```
                         Write Lock successfully installed.
***** Blocked Write Commands *****
CMD: a:\TEST-HDL.EXE SWB-40 McMillan JRL w F6 6F 64 E3 1F
Case: SWB-40
Command set: Write
Date: Sun Aug 31 09:27:21 2003


Version: @(#) test-hdl.cpp Version 1.1 Created 08/23/03 at 10:13:51
        @(#) wb-defs.h Version 1.2 Created 08/31/03 at 08:18:19
        Compiled on Aug 31 2003 at 08:10:54
Operator: JRL
Host: McMillan
Number of drives 5, Drives: F6 6F 64 E3 1F
      Case  Cmd Drv Action  Stat Cry Count Cmd Name
  0 SWB-40 <03> 80 Blocked 0000 Off      0  WriteSectors
  1 SWB-40 <0B> 80 Blocked 0000 Off      0  WriteLong
  2 SWB-40 <43> 80 Blocked 0000 Off      0  ExtWrite
Results for SWB-40 category w on drive 80 All commands blocked (3 of 3)
  0 SWB-40 <03> 81 Blocked 0000 Off      0  WriteSectors
  1 SWB-40 <0B> 81 Blocked 0000 Off      0  WriteLong
  2 SWB-40 <43> 81 Blocked 0000 Off      0  ExtWrite
Results for SWB-40 category w on drive 81 All commands blocked (3 of 3)
  0 SWB-40 <03> 82 Allowed 0000 Off      1  WriteSectors
  1 SWB-40 <0B> 82 Allowed 0000 Off      1  WriteLong
  2 SWB-40 <43> 82 Allowed 0000 Off      1  ExtWrite
Results for SWB-40 category w on drive 82 No commands blocked (0 of 3)
  0 SWB-40 <03> 83 Allowed 0000 Off      1  WriteSectors
  1 SWB-40 <0B> 83 Allowed 0000 Off      1  WriteLong
  2 SWB-40 <43> 83 Allowed 0000 Off      1  ExtWrite
Results for SWB-40 category w on drive 83 No commands blocked (0 of 3)
  0 SWB-40 <03> 84 Allowed 0000 Off      1  WriteSectors
  1 SWB-40 <0B> 84 Allowed 0000 Off      1  WriteLong
  2 SWB-40 <43> 84 Allowed 0000 Off      1  ExtWrite
Results for SWB-40 category w on drive 84 No commands blocked (0 of 3)
Summary: 15 sent, 6 blocked, 9 not blocked



Number of Commands not blocked (should total to 9)
Drive  Count
  80      0
  81      0
  82      3
  83      3
  84      3
***** Uninstall HDL Log *****
HDL -- Int_13 Hard Disk Write Lock V0.8 021126 (c)RCMP 1993-2002
        ---- Royal  Canadian  Mounted  Police  ----
        UNAUTHORIZED  USE / DISTRIBUTION  PROHIBITED


        Licensee: US Dept. Commerce / NIST S/W Testing
        5  Hard-Disks reported by Int_13h
        Write Lock now non-removable!
***** Test Harness Log *****
CMD: a:\TEST-HDL.EXE SWB-40 McMillan JRL a F6 6F 64 E3 1F
Case: SWB-40
Command set: All
Date: Sun Aug 31 09:27:36 2003


Version: @(#) test-hdl.cpp Version 1.1 Created 08/23/03 at 10:13:51
        @(#) wb-defs.h Version 1.2 Created 08/31/03 at 08:18:19
        Compiled on Aug 31 2003 at 08:10:54
Operator: JRL
Host: McMillan
Number of drives 5, Drives: F6 6F 64 E3 1F
Warning: non-zero tally (3) for drive 82 (reboot to clear)
Warning: non-zero tally (3) for drive 83 (reboot to clear)
Warning: non-zero tally (3) for drive 84 (reboot to clear)
      Case  Cmd Drv Action  Stat Cry Count Cmd Name
  0 SWB-40 <00> 80 Allowed 0000 Off      1  Reset
  1 SWB-40 <0C> 80 Allowed 0000 Off      1  SeekDrive
  2 SWB-40 <0D> 80 Allowed 0000 Off      1  AltReset
  3 SWB-40 <11> 80 Blocked 0000 Off      0  Recalibrate
  4 SWB-40 <47> 80 Blocked 0000 Off      0  ExtendedSeek
```

```
Results for SWB-40 category c on drive 80 Not all commands blocked (2
of 5)
    0 SWB-40 <00> 81 Allowed 0000 Off     1   Reset
    1 SWB-40 <0C> 81 Allowed 0000 Off     1   SeekDrive
    2 SWB-40 <0D> 81 Allowed 0000 Off     1   AltReset
    3 SWB-40 <11> 81 Blocked 0000 Off     0   Recalibrate
    4 SWB-40 <47> 81 Blocked 0000 Off     0   ExtendedSeek
Results for SWB-40 category c on drive 81 Not all commands blocked (2
of 5)
    0 SWB-40 <00> 82 Allowed 0000 Off     1   Reset
    1 SWB-40 <0C> 82 Allowed 0000 Off     1   SeekDrive
    2 SWB-40 <0D> 82 Allowed 0000 Off     1   AltReset
    3 SWB-40 <11> 82 Allowed 0000 Off     1   Recalibrate
    4 SWB-40 <47> 82 Allowed 0000 Off     1   ExtendedSeek
Results for SWB-40 category c on drive 82 No commands blocked (0 of 5)
    0 SWB-40 <00> 83 Allowed 0000 Off     1   Reset
    1 SWB-40 <0C> 83 Allowed 0000 Off     1   SeekDrive
    2 SWB-40 <0D> 83 Allowed 0000 Off     1   AltReset
    3 SWB-40 <11> 83 Allowed 0000 Off     1   Recalibrate
    4 SWB-40 <47> 83 Allowed 0000 Off     1   ExtendedSeek
Results for SWB-40 category c on drive 83 No commands blocked (0 of 5)
    0 SWB-40 <00> 84 Allowed 0000 Off     1   Reset
    1 SWB-40 <0C> 84 Allowed 0000 Off     1   SeekDrive
    2 SWB-40 <0D> 84 Allowed 0000 Off     1   AltReset
    3 SWB-40 <11> 84 Allowed 0000 Off     1   Recalibrate
    4 SWB-40 <47> 84 Allowed 0000 Off     1   ExtendedSeek
Results for SWB-40 category c on drive 84 No commands blocked (0 of 5)
Summary: 25 sent, 4 blocked, 21 not blocked

    0 SWB-40 <01> 80 Allowed 0000 Off     1   GetLastStatus
    1 SWB-40 <04> 80 Allowed 0000 Off     1   VerifySectors
    2 SWB-40 <08> 80 Allowed 0000 Off     1   ReadDriveParms
    3 SWB-40 <10> 80 Allowed 0000 Off     1   TestDriveReady
    4 SWB-40 <15> 80 Allowed 0000 Off     1   ReadDriveType
    5 SWB-40 <41> 80 Allowed 0000 Off     1   CheckForExtensions
    6 SWB-40 <44> 80 Allowed 0000 Off     1   VerifySectors
    7 SWB-40 <48> 80 Allowed 0000 Off     1   GetDriveParms
Results for SWB-40 category i on drive 80 No commands blocked (0 of 8)
    0 SWB-40 <01> 81 Allowed 0000 Off     1   GetLastStatus
    1 SWB-40 <04> 81 Allowed 0000 Off     1   VerifySectors
    2 SWB-40 <08> 81 Allowed 0000 Off     1   ReadDriveParms
    3 SWB-40 <10> 81 Allowed 0000 Off     1   TestDriveReady
    4 SWB-40 <15> 81 Allowed 0000 Off     1   ReadDriveType
    5 SWB-40 <41> 81 Allowed 0000 Off     1   CheckForExtensions
    6 SWB-40 <44> 81 Allowed 0000 Off     1   VerifySectors
    7 SWB-40 <48> 81 Allowed 0000 Off     1   GetDriveParms
Results for SWB-40 category i on drive 81 No commands blocked (0 of 8)
    0 SWB-40 <01> 82 Allowed 0000 Off     1   GetLastStatus
    1 SWB-40 <04> 82 Allowed 0000 Off     1   VerifySectors
    2 SWB-40 <08> 82 Allowed 0000 Off     1   ReadDriveParms
    3 SWB-40 <10> 82 Allowed 0000 Off     1   TestDriveReady
    4 SWB-40 <15> 82 Allowed 0000 Off     1   ReadDriveType
    5 SWB-40 <41> 82 Allowed 0000 Off     1   CheckForExtensions
    6 SWB-40 <44> 82 Allowed 0000 Off     1   VerifySectors
    7 SWB-40 <48> 82 Allowed 0000 Off     1   GetDriveParms
Results for SWB-40 category i on drive 82 No commands blocked (0 of 8)
    0 SWB-40 <01> 83 Allowed 0000 Off     1   GetLastStatus
    1 SWB-40 <04> 83 Allowed 0000 Off     1   VerifySectors
    2 SWB-40 <08> 83 Allowed 0000 Off     1   ReadDriveParms
    3 SWB-40 <10> 83 Allowed 0000 Off     1   TestDriveReady
    4 SWB-40 <15> 83 Allowed 0000 Off     1   ReadDriveType
    5 SWB-40 <41> 83 Allowed 0000 Off     1   CheckForExtensions
    6 SWB-40 <44> 83 Allowed 0000 Off     1   VerifySectors
    7 SWB-40 <48> 83 Allowed 0000 Off     1   GetDriveParms
Results for SWB-40 category i on drive 83 No commands blocked (0 of 8)
    0 SWB-40 <01> 84 Allowed 0000 Off     1   GetLastStatus
    1 SWB-40 <04> 84 Allowed 0000 Off     1   VerifySectors
    2 SWB-40 <08> 84 Allowed 0000 Off     1   ReadDriveParms
    3 SWB-40 <10> 84 Allowed 0000 Off     1   TestDriveReady
    4 SWB-40 <15> 84 Allowed 0000 Off     1   ReadDriveType
    5 SWB-40 <41> 84 Allowed 0000 Off     1   CheckForExtensions
    6 SWB-40 <44> 84 Allowed 0000 Off     1   VerifySectors
    7 SWB-40 <48> 84 Allowed 0000 Off     1   GetDriveParms
```

```
Results for SWB-40 category i on drive 84 No commands blocked (0 of 8)
Summary: 40 sent, 0 blocked, 40 not blocked

   0  SWB-40 <02> 80 Allowed 0000 Off     1  ReadSectors
   1  SWB-40 <0A> 80 Allowed 0000 Off     1  ReadLong
   2  SWB-40 <42> 80 Allowed 0000 Off     1  ExtRead
Results for SWB-40 category r on drive 80 No commands blocked (0 of 3)
   0  SWB-40 <02> 81 Allowed 0000 Off     1  ReadSectors
   1  SWB-40 <0A> 81 Allowed 0000 Off     1  ReadLong
   2  SWB-40 <42> 81 Allowed 0000 Off     1  ExtRead
Results for SWB-40 category r on drive 81 No commands blocked (0 of 3)
   0  SWB-40 <02> 82 Allowed 0000 Off     1  ReadSectors
   1  SWB-40 <0A> 82 Allowed 0000 Off     1  ReadLong
   2  SWB-40 <42> 82 Allowed 0000 Off     1  ExtRead
Results for SWB-40 category r on drive 82 No commands blocked (0 of 3)
   0  SWB-40 <02> 83 Allowed 0000 Off     1  ReadSectors
   1  SWB-40 <0A> 83 Allowed 0000 Off     1  ReadLong
   2  SWB-40 <42> 83 Allowed 0000 Off     1  ExtRead
Results for SWB-40 category r on drive 83 No commands blocked (0 of 3)
   0  SWB-40 <02> 84 Allowed 0000 Off     1  ReadSectors
   1  SWB-40 <0A> 84 Allowed 0000 Off     1  ReadLong
   2  SWB-40 <42> 84 Allowed 0000 Off     1  ExtRead
Results for SWB-40 category r on drive 84 No commands blocked (0 of 3)
Summary: 15 sent, 0 blocked, 15 not blocked

   0  SWB-40 <03> 80 Blocked 0000 Off     0  WriteSectors
   1  SWB-40 <0B> 80 Blocked 0000 Off     0  WriteLong
   2  SWB-40 <43> 80 Blocked 0000 Off     0  ExtWrite
Results for SWB-40 category w on drive 80 All commands blocked (3 of 3)
   0  SWB-40 <03> 81 Blocked 0000 Off     0  WriteSectors
   1  SWB-40 <0B> 81 Blocked 0000 Off     0  WriteLong
   2  SWB-40 <43> 81 Blocked 0000 Off     0  ExtWrite
Results for SWB-40 category w on drive 81 All commands blocked (3 of 3)
   0  SWB-40 <03> 82 Allowed 0000 Off     2  WriteSectors
   1  SWB-40 <0B> 82 Allowed 0000 Off     2  WriteLong
   2  SWB-40 <43> 82 Allowed 0000 Off     2  ExtWrite
Results for SWB-40 category w on drive 82 No commands blocked (0 of 3)
   0  SWB-40 <03> 83 Allowed 0000 Off     2  WriteSectors
   1  SWB-40 <0B> 83 Allowed 0000 Off     2  WriteLong
   2  SWB-40 <43> 83 Allowed 0000 Off     2  ExtWrite
Results for SWB-40 category w on drive 83 No commands blocked (0 of 3)
   0  SWB-40 <03> 84 Allowed 0000 Off     2  WriteSectors
   1  SWB-40 <0B> 84 Allowed 0000 Off     2  WriteLong
   2  SWB-40 <43> 84 Allowed 0000 Off     2  ExtWrite
Results for SWB-40 category w on drive 84 No commands blocked (0 of 3)
Summary: 15 sent, 6 blocked, 9 not blocked

   0  SWB-40 <05> 80 Blocked 0000 Off     0  FormatTrack
   1  SWB-40 <06> 80 Blocked 0000 Off     0  FormatBadSectors
   2  SWB-40 <07> 80 Blocked 0000 Off     0  FormatCyl
   3  SWB-40 <09> 80 Blocked 0000 Off     0  InitDriveParms
   4  SWB-40 <0E> 80 Blocked 0000 Off     0  DiagnosticESDI
   5  SWB-40 <0F> 80 Blocked 0000 Off     0  DiagnosticESDI
   6  SWB-40 <12> 80 Blocked 0000 Off     0  DiagnosticRAM
   7  SWB-40 <13> 80 Blocked 0000 Off     0  DiagnosticDrive
   8  SWB-40 <14> 80 Blocked 0000 Off     0  DiagnosticCTL
Results for SWB-40 category x on drive 80 All commands blocked (9 of 9)
   0  SWB-40 <05> 81 Blocked 0000 Off     0  FormatTrack
   1  SWB-40 <06> 81 Blocked 0000 Off     0  FormatBadSectors
   2  SWB-40 <07> 81 Blocked 0000 Off     0  FormatCyl
   3  SWB-40 <09> 81 Blocked 0000 Off     0  InitDriveParms
   4  SWB-40 <0E> 81 Blocked 0000 Off     0  DiagnosticESDI
   5  SWB-40 <0F> 81 Blocked 0000 Off     0  DiagnosticESDI
   6  SWB-40 <12> 81 Blocked 0000 Off     0  DiagnosticRAM
   7  SWB-40 <13> 81 Blocked 0000 Off     0  DiagnosticDrive
   8  SWB-40 <14> 81 Blocked 0000 Off     0  DiagnosticCTL
Results for SWB-40 category x on drive 81 All commands blocked (9 of 9)
   0  SWB-40 <05> 82 Allowed 0000 Off     1  FormatTrack
   1  SWB-40 <06> 82 Allowed 0000 Off     1  FormatBadSectors
   2  SWB-40 <07> 82 Allowed 0000 Off     1  FormatCyl
   3  SWB-40 <09> 82 Allowed 0000 Off     1  InitDriveParms
   4  SWB-40 <0E> 82 Allowed 0000 Off     1  DiagnosticESDI
   5  SWB-40 <0F> 82 Allowed 0000 Off     1  DiagnosticESDI
```

```
   6 SWB-40 <12> 82 Allowed 0000 Off        1   DiagnosticRAM
   7 SWB-40 <13> 82 Allowed 0000 Off        1   DiagnosticDrive
   8 SWB-40 <14> 82 Allowed 0000 Off        1   DiagnosticCTL
Results for SWB-40 category x on drive 82 No commands blocked (0 of 9)
   0 SWB-40 <05> 83 Allowed 0000 Off        1   FormatTrack
   1 SWB-40 <06> 83 Allowed 0000 Off        1   FormatBadSectors
   2 SWB-40 <07> 83 Allowed 0000 Off        1   FormatCyl
   3 SWB-40 <09> 83 Allowed 0000 Off        1   InitDriveParms
   4 SWB-40 <0E> 83 Allowed 0000 Off        1   DiagnosticESDI
   5 SWB-40 <0F> 83 Allowed 0000 Off        1   DiagnosticESDI
   6 SWB-40 <12> 83 Allowed 0000 Off        1   DiagnosticRAM
   7 SWB-40 <13> 83 Allowed 0000 Off        1   DiagnosticDrive
   8 SWB-40 <14> 83 Allowed 0000 Off        1   DiagnosticCTL
Results for SWB-40 category x on drive 83 No commands blocked (0 of 9)
   0 SWB-40 <05> 84 Allowed 0000 Off        1   FormatTrack
   1 SWB-40 <06> 84 Allowed 0000 Off        1   FormatBadSectors
   2 SWB-40 <07> 84 Allowed 0000 Off        1   FormatCyl
   3 SWB-40 <09> 84 Allowed 0000 Off        1   InitDriveParms
   4 SWB-40 <0E> 84 Allowed 0000 Off        1   DiagnosticESDI
   5 SWB-40 <0F> 84 Allowed 0000 Off        1   DiagnosticESDI
   6 SWB-40 <12> 84 Allowed 0000 Off        1   DiagnosticRAM
   7 SWB-40 <13> 84 Allowed 0000 Off        1   DiagnosticDrive
   8 SWB-40 <14> 84 Allowed 0000 Off        1   DiagnosticCTL
Results for SWB-40 category x on drive 84 No commands blocked (0 of 9)
Summary: 45 sent, 18 blocked, 27 not blocked

   0 SWB-40 <16> 80 Blocked 0000 Off        0   Undefined
          ...

          misc commands 17-FD results omitted

          see log files for full results


          ...

226 SWB-40 <FE> 80 Blocked 0000 Off        0   Undefined
227 SWB-40 <FF> 80 Blocked 0000 Off        0   Undefined
Results for SWB-40 category m on drive 80 All commands blocked (228 of
228)
   0 SWB-40 <16> 81 Blocked 0000 Off        0   Undefined
          ...

          misc commands 17-FD results omitted

          see log files for full results


          ...

226 SWB-40 <FE> 81 Blocked 0000 Off        0   Undefined
227 SWB-40 <FF> 81 Blocked 0000 Off        0   Undefined
Results for SWB-40 category m on drive 81 All commands blocked (228 of
228)
   0 SWB-40 <16> 82 Allowed 0000 Off        1   Undefined
          ...

          misc commands 17-FD results omitted

          see log files for full results


          ...

226 SWB-40 <FE> 82 Allowed 0000 Off        1   Undefined
227 SWB-40 <FF> 82 Allowed 0000 Off        1   Undefined
Results for SWB-40 category m on drive 82 No commands blocked (0 of
228)
   0 SWB-40 <16> 83 Allowed 0000 Off        1   Undefined
          ...

          misc commands 17-FD results omitted

          see log files for full results


          ...
```

```
226 SWB-40 <FE> 83 Allowed 0000 Off     1 Undefined
227 SWB-40 <FF> 83 Allowed 0000 Off     1 Undefined
Results for SWB-40 category m on drive 83 No commands blocked (0 of
228)
  0 SWB-40 <16> 84 Allowed 0000 Off     1 Undefined

            ...

        misc commands 17-FD results omitted

        see log files for full results

    ...

226 SWB-40 <FE> 84 Allowed 0000 Off     1 Undefined
227 SWB-40 <FF> 84 Allowed 0000 Off     1 Undefined
Results for SWB-40 category m on drive 84 No commands blocked (0 of
228)
Summary: 1140 sent, 456 blocked, 684 not blocked
```

Results:

Assertion	Expected Results	Actual Results
AM-07	Tool active message	Tool active message
AM-08	5 drives identified	5 drives identified
AM-09	Drive 80 is protected	Drive 80 is protected
AM-09	Drive 81 is protected	Drive 81 is protected
AM-09	Drive 82 is unprotected	Drive 82 is unprotected
AM-09	Drive 83 is unprotected	Drive 83 is unprotected
AM-09	Drive 84 is unprotected	Drive 84 is unprotected
AM-10	484 Commands return success	484 Commands return success
AO-09	SWB not removed	Write Lock now non-removable!

Analysis: SWB-40 Expected results achieved

About the National Institute of Justice

NIJ is the research, development, and evaluation agency of the U.S. Department of Justice. The Institute provides objective, independent, evidence-based knowledge and tools to enhance the administration of justice and public safety. NIJ's principal authorities are derived from the Omnibus Crime Control and Safe Streets Act of 1968, as amended (see 42 U.S.C. §§ 3721–3723).

The NIJ Director is appointed by the President and confirmed by the Senate. The Director establishes the Institute's objectives, guided by the priorities of the Office of Justice Programs, the U.S. Department of Justice, and the needs of the field. The Institute actively solicits the views of criminal justice and other professionals and researchers to inform its search for the knowledge and tools to guide policy and practice.

Strategic Goals

NIJ has seven strategic goals grouped into three categories:

Creating relevant knowledge and tools

1. Partner with State and local practitioners and policymakers to identify social science research and technology needs.
2. Create scientific, relevant, and reliable knowledge—with a particular emphasis on terrorism, violent crime, drugs and crime, cost-effectiveness, and community-based efforts—to enhance the administration of justice and public safety.
3. Develop affordable and effective tools and technologies to enhance the administration of justice and public safety.

Dissemination

4. Disseminate relevant knowledge and information to practitioners and policymakers in an understandable, timely, and concise manner.
5. Act as an honest broker to identify the information, tools, and technologies that respond to the needs of stakeholders.

Agency management

6. Practice fairness and openness in the research and development process.
7. Ensure professionalism, excellence, accountability, cost-effectiveness, and integrity in the management and conduct of NIJ activities and programs.

Program Areas

In addressing these strategic challenges, the Institute is involved in the following program areas: crime control and prevention, including policing; drugs and crime; justice systems and offender behavior, including corrections; violence and victimization; communications and information technologies; critical incident response; investigative and forensic sciences, including DNA; less-than-lethal technologies; officer protection; education and training technologies; testing and standards; technology assistance to law enforcement and corrections agencies; field testing of promising programs; and international crime control.

In addition to sponsoring research and development and technology assistance, NIJ evaluates programs, policies, and technologies. NIJ communicates its research and evaluation findings through conferences and print and electronic media.

To find out more about the National Institute of Justice, please contact:

National Criminal Justice
 Reference Service
P.O. Box 6000
Rockville, MD 20849–6000
800–851–3420
e-mail: askncjrs@ncjrs.org